Activities
for a
Differentiated
Classroom

Developed by

Wendy Conklin, M.A.

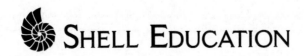

SHELL EDUCATION

Consultant

Chandra C. Prough, M.S.Ed.
National Board Certified
Newport-Mesa
Unified School District

Contributing Authors

Kelly Jones
Stephanie Kuligowski

Publishing Credits

Dona Herweck Rice, *Editor-in-Chief;* Lee Aucoin, *Creative Director;*
Don Tran, *Print Production Manager;* Timothy J. Bradley, *Illustration Manager;*
Chris McIntyre, M.A.Ed., *Editorial Director;* Sara Johnson, M.S.Ed., *Senior Editor;*
Aubrie Nielsen, M.S., *Associate Education Editor;* Robin Erickson, *Interior Layout Designer;*
Juan Chavolla, *Production Artist;* Ana Clark, *Illustrator;* Stephanie Reid, *Photo Editor;*
Corinne Burton, M.S.Ed., *Publisher*

Image Credits

p.54 Radlovsk Yaroslav/Shutterstock; p.55 Constance McGuire/iStockphoto; p.56 ImageryMajestic/Shutterstock; p.138 (George Washington) Library of Congress [LC-DIG-ppmsca-19171], (Paul Revere) Library of Congress [LC-USZ62-7407], (John Hancock) Library of Congress [LC-USZ62-45235], (Benjamin Franklin) Library of Congress [LC-USZ62-37337], (Martha Washington) Library of Congress [LC-USZC2-3273]; p.156 Getty Images; p.162 Library of Congress [LC-USZC4-2399]; p.165 Library of Congress [LC-USZ62-97946]

Shell Education

5301 Oceanus Drive
Huntington Beach, CA 92649-1030
http://www.shelleducation.com
ISBN 978-1-4258-0737-5
© 2011 Shell Educational Publishing, Inc.
Reprinted 2013

Table of Contents

Understanding Differentiation

As I conduct workshops with teachers of all ages and grade levels, I hear a familiar tune: *Differentiating curriculum is worrisome and stressful.* I believe this is due to the fact that teachers do not know how to begin differentiating. Their administrators tell them that they must differentiate, but teachers are overwhelmed with the task of doing it because there is not a clear explanation of what to do. Teachers know the theory. They know they need to do it. They just do not know *how* to do it.

The right way to differentiate depends on the unique students in a classroom. To successfully differentiate, teachers must first know their students. Knowing what academic level students are at helps us understand where to begin. When we have students who do not succeed, we find out why they are not succeeding. Then, we look for the type of support that they need to help them learn specific concepts. We make adjustments when students have trouble comprehending material. We look for new ways to present information, new manipulatives that make sense, and opportunities to provide additional support. As our struggling students grow, we can then scaffold the amount of support that we provide so that students continue to grow instead of leaning too heavily on that support. Differentiation is about meeting the needs of *all* students and providing the right amount of challenge for *all* students.

What Should I Differentiate and Why?

Many teachers have heard the terms *content*, *process*, and *product* when it comes to differentiating curriculum, but few have the time to ponder how these words apply to what they do in their classrooms. Below is a chart that briefly defines how we differentiate and why we differentiate.

Differentiating Curriculum

How	Why
Vary the Content (what is taught)	**Readiness** (students are not at the same academic level)
Vary the Process (how it is taught)	**Learning Styles** (students prefer different ways of learning)
Vary the Product (what students produce)	**Interests** (students have different passions)

Differentiation Strategies in This Book

What Differentiation Strategies Can I Use?

Each book in the *Activities for a Differentiated Classroom* series introduces a selection of differentiation strategies. Each lesson in this book uses one of the six differentiation strategies outlined below. The strategies are used across different curriculum areas and topics to provide you with multiple real-world examples.

Differentiation Strategy		Lessons in This Book
	Tiered Assignments	• Book in a Day—*Language Arts* • Exploring Volume—*Mathematics* • Rock Investigation—*Science* • The Civil War—*Social Studies*
	Tiered Graphic Organizers	• Writing with Details—*Language Arts* • Equivalent Fractions—*Mathematics* • Animal Adaptations—*Science* • Revolutionary Social Networking—*Social Studies*
	Bloom's Taxonomy	• Literature Response—*Language Arts* • Introducing Algebra—*Mathematics* • Inherited Traits—*Science* • Reconstruction—*Social Studies*
	Menu of Options	• Persuasive Practice—*Language Arts* • Geometry Wrap-Up—*Mathematics* • Forces and Motion—*Science* • Colonial America—*Social Studies*
	Choices Board	• Identifying Genres—*Language Arts* • Number Sense—*Mathematics* • Food Chains—*Science* • Declaration of Independence—*Social Studies*
	Leveled Learning Contracts	• Making Inferences—*Language Arts* • Long Division Algorithm—*Mathematics* • The Scientific Method—*Science* • Westward Expansion—*Social Studies*

Tiered Assignments

One way to ensure that all students in a classroom advance—using the same skills and ideas regardless of readiness levels—is to tier lessons. Often referred to as *scaffolding*, tiered assignments offer multilevel activities based on key skills at differing levels of complexity. One example of this is leveled reading texts. All students can learn about the Civil War by reading texts that are leveled according to the different reading abilities in the classroom. You can also provide comprehension questions that are leveled. Each student comes away with essential grade-appropriate skills in addition to being sufficiently challenged. The entire class works toward one goal (learning about the Civil War), but the path to that goal depends on each student's readiness level.

So, how do you tier lessons?

- **Pick the skill, concept, or strategy that needs to be learned.** For example, a key concept would be using reading skills and strategies to understand and interpret a variety of informational texts.

- **Think of an activity that teaches this skill, concept, or strategy.** For this example, you could have students summarize the information and include a main idea in the summary.

- **Assess students.** You may already have a good idea of your students' readiness levels, but you can further assess them through classroom discussions, quizzes, tests, or journal entries. These assessments can tell you if students are above grade level, on grade level, or below grade level.

- **Take another look at the activity you developed.** How complex is it? Where would it fit on a continuum scale? Is it appropriate for above-grade-level learners, on-grade-level learners, below-grade-level learners, or English language learners?

- **Modify the activity to meet the needs of the other learners in the class.** Try to get help from the specialists in your school for English language learners, special education students, and gifted learners. For this example, summarizing with a main idea would be appropriate for on-grade-level students. Above-grade-level students should include supporting details in their summaries. The below-grade-level students will need a few examples provided for their summaries. English language learners will begin with the same examples given to below-grade-level students so that they understand what is expected of them. Then, they will summarize information verbally to you.

Remember, just because students are above grade level does not mean that they should be given more work. And, just because students are below grade level does not mean that they should be given less work. Tiered lessons are differentiated by varying the *complexity*, not necessarily the *quantity* of work required for the assignment. Likewise, all tiered activities should be interesting and engaging.

Differentiation Strategies in This Book (cont.)

Tiered Graphic Organizers

One way to improve the learning and performance of diverse students across grade levels in a wide range of content areas is by utilizing graphic organizers in classroom lessons. Graphic organizers are visual representations that help students gather and sort information, see patterns and relationships, clarify concepts, and organize information. Graphic organizers have a way of connecting several pieces of isolated information by taking new information and fitting it into an existing framework. Old information is retrieved in the process, and the new information is attached. By using graphic organizers in the classroom, teachers are helping students make connections and assimilate new information with what they already know.

Understanding how the brain works helps us understand why graphic organizers are valuable tools for learning. Educational brain research says that our brains seek patterns so that information can become meaningful. In her book, Karen Olsen (1995) states, "From brain research we have come to understand that the brain is a pattern-seeking device in search of meaning and that learning is the acquisition of mental programs for using what we understand." Other researchers believe that graphic organizers are one of the most powerful ways to build semantic memories (Sprenger 1999). Eric Jensen (1998) states that semantic memory is "activated by association, similarities, or contrasts." Graphic organizers assist students with such necessary connections.

The brain does this by storing information similar to how a graphic organizer shows information. It screens large amounts of information and looks for patterns that are linked together. The brain is able to extract meaning more easily from a visual format like a graphic organizer than from written words on a page. Graphic organizers not only help students manage information, they also offer information in a way that students can understand at a glance. When these connections happen, the brain transfers the information from short-term memory to long-term memory. This means that teachers who use graphic organizers help their students manage all the information that they are presented with each day.

Because students are at different readiness levels, it makes sense to differentiate lessons with tiered graphic organizers. Some teachers worry that students will copy from other students who have additional examples on their graphic organizers. They also note that some of their students do not like to be singled out with modified work. This can be resolved by assigning groups different types of graphic organizers within one lesson. An example of this would be to give one group Venn diagrams, another group T-charts, and a third group matrices. The information can still be scaffolded as needed, but more discreetly because the organizers are different.

Bloom's Taxonomy

In 1956, educator Benjamin Bloom worked with a group of educational psychologists to classify levels of cognitive thinking. Bloom's Taxonomy has been used in classrooms for more than 40 years as a hierarchy of questions that progress from less to more complex. The progression allows teachers to identify the levels at which students are thinking. It also provides a framework for introducing a variety of questions to all students.

In the 1990s, cognitive psychologist Lorin Anderson, a former student of Bloom, led a group of researchers to revise and update the taxonomy for the twenty-first century. There are two main changes. One involves changing the nouns to verbs. For example, instead of *comprehension* (a noun), the word is *understanding* (a verb). Also, the hierarchy of the last two levels of Bloom's Taxonomy changed from *evaluation* to *creating* as the highest form of thinking (Anderson and Krathwohl 2001).

Bloom's Taxonomy

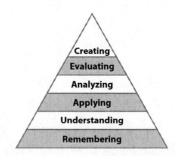

Bloom's Taxonomy (Revised)

Some teachers view Bloom's Taxonomy as a ladder. They think that all students have to begin at the bottom with *remembering* questions and then progressively work their way up to the *creating* questions. It is natural for most teachers to only ask lower-level questions and assign lower-level activities. *Who is this? What is that?* Instead, this taxonomy should serve as a guide to help teachers purposefully plan for higher-order thinking. All students, regardless of readiness levels, need to develop higher-order thinking skills. At times, it is necessary to ask lower-level questions when content is very new, even of above-grade-level students. These students typically need questions that challenge them to use higher-level thinking skills. Otherwise, they might become bored answering questions that they already understand and do not have to think about. It is just as necessary to ask below-grade-level students to evaluate a statement. However, the language of the higher-level question might need to be scaffolded for struggling students and for English language learners.

Bloom's Taxonomy is a useful model for categorizing test questions and designing lessons for your class. It differentiates the curriculum easily. Students who need background information can complete the remembering and understanding activities. Students who can access prior knowledge can do the applying or analyzing activities. Students who need a challenge can work on activities that involve evaluating and creating.

Differentiation Strategies in This Book (cont.)

Menu of Options

Providing students the opportunity to choose what activity they want to do increases their level of interest in what they are doing or learning. However, many students do not often get the chance to make choices about their work. It can be challenging and time-consuming for teachers to develop a variety of engaging activities. Yet offering options is essential to getting students interested and motivated in learning. When students are involved in something of their own choosing, they are more engaged in the learning process (Bess 1997; Brandt 1998).

Choices in the classroom can be offered in a variety of ways. Students can choose what they will learn (content), how they will learn (process), and how they will show what they have learned (product). A menu of options is a strategy that differentiates product by giving students the opportunity to choose from a list of highly engaging activities.

The menu of options strategy works well for many reasons. First, it operates much like a menu from a restaurant. A person looking at a menu sees all the choices. Some cost more and some cost less. No one likes going to a restaurant and being told what to eat. People enjoy choosing what they prefer from the menu. In the same way, a menu of options offers students many different projects from which to choose. These projects are assigned various point values. The point values depend on the amount of work or detail involved in the project. Students must earn a set number of points determined by the teacher, but they can choose which activities they want to complete. Any kind of point system can be used. For example, basic projects that do not take much time can be worth 10 points. Projects that take a moderate amount of time and energy can be worth 30 points. Projects that are very time-consuming can be worth 50 points. If the students need to complete 80 points total, they can get to that total number in many different ways. They may choose a 50-point project and a 30-point project. Or, they may choose two 30-point projects and two 10-point projects.

Secondly, a menu of options is effective because the freedom of choice allows students to complete projects that are of interest to them. This increases the chance that the students will produce high-quality products. Students like to feel in control. When given a list to choose from, students often choose projects that they like or that fit their learning styles. If the teacher provides enough variety, then all students can find projects that they feel passionate about.

As an alternative to creating a menu of options based on point systems, a teacher can create three or four sections on a menu of options and ask students to choose one project from each section. This strategy is helpful when there are a particular set of concepts that the teacher needs to be sure that students have learned.

Choices Board

Everyone loves to make his or her own choices. Getting the chance to choose what we want increases the chances that we are actually interested in what we are doing or learning. Sadly, students do not always get the chance to make choices. Curriculum plans demand that teachers teach a certain way or about a certain topic. Students have to follow along and pretend to be interested. This does not fool most teachers. One key to getting students engaged in learning is to pique their interests by offering choices. It has been noted that when students are engaged in something of interest or choice, they are more engaged in the learning process (Bess 1997; Brandt 1998). Choices can be given in a variety of ways in a classroom. Choices can be given in what students will learn (content), how they will learn (process), and how they will show what they have learned (product).

Equally important is giving students academically appropriate assignments. Tiering or leveling assignments will ensure that students work on parallel tasks designed to have varied levels of depth, complexity, and abstractness along with varied degrees of scaffolding, support, and direction, depending on each student and the topic. All students work toward one goal, concept, or outcome, but the lesson is tiered to allow for different levels of readiness and performance. As students work, they build on their prior knowledge and understanding. Tiered assignments are productive because all students work on similar tasks that provide individual challenges. Students are motivated to be successful according to their own readiness levels as well as their own learning preferences.

Choices boards combine both choices and tiering by giving students the opportunities to choose leveled activities from a larger list. The difficulty levels of the activities vary.

△ above-grade-level students (shown by a triangle)

□ on-grade-level students (shown by a square)

○ below-grade-level students (shown by a circle)

☆ English language learners (shown by a star)

There should be at least two of each leveled activity so that students have an option. A teacher controls the levels of the activities, while students control which activity they will complete within that level. For example, when giving an on-grade-level student an assignment, the teacher may tell the student to choose any square activity from the choices board, and then challenge himself or herself by choosing a triangle activity.

Differentiation Strategies in This Book *(cont.)*

Leveled Learning Contracts

Leveled learning contracts are individualized, independent agreements between the teacher and students. Leveled learning contracts provide structure to students while at the same time allowing them to think critically and work on complex ideas at their own readiness levels. They encourage students to develop independence and time-management skills (Winebrenner 1992). Often teachers set up leveled learning contracts so that students have the opportunity to select from a list of choices. Leveled learning contracts are also flexible. Teachers can use leveled learning contracts in the everyday classroom with all students. Topics can be the same or varied, but the way students learn and show what they have learned can differ according to abilities, learning styles, and readiness levels. Leveled learning contracts can also be used for remedial help. This gives students the necessary time to spend on topics that are confusing at first. Leveled learning contracts can be used as enrichment options. This will provide some students the opportunity to delve deeper into topics and spend extra time on a class topic. Or, the contracts can be used for acceleration if the school district is committed to continually providing accelerated curriculum to students who need it.

After determining the assignments and projects that the learning contracts should contain, meet with students individually or in small groups to explain the contracts. It is the teacher's responsibility to set up each contract so that students will learn the needed skills. These skills should be listed on the contract along with the ways in which students will apply those skills. Students, however, take on the responsibility for their own learning. The contract must be signed by both the student and the teacher. Some teachers also choose to use learning contracts in order to allow advanced students to contract out of whole-class lessons. If above-grade-level students already know the content, you can write a learning contract with them to give them focused tasks related to the curriculum. They can then complete the learning contract instead of participating in lessons based on content that they already know (Winebrenner 1992).

It is also helpful if an assessment and a rubric are included with the leveled learning contracts. A rubric will help students to know how they will be evaluated on their contract projects. Grades can be broken down into a few different categories. One grade might be based on the student's work ethic. Did he or she follow the rules on the contracts? Did he or she work toward goals? Another grade is based on the actual assignments. Select one or two assignments and check them for accuracy, quality, and completion. The last grade could be based on an assessment. Allow students to complete self-assessments as well as peer assessments on one or two assignments.

As a final note, teachers should set up periodic appointments with students to check their progress. Teachers might also have students work with partners or groups to monitor one another's daily progress. This will allow time for teachers to work with small groups or individual students who are having trouble.

Grouping Students

What Grouping Strategies Can I Use?

There are many variables that a teacher must consider when grouping students to create a successful learning environment. These variables include gender, chemistry between students, social maturity, academic readiness, and special needs. Some students will work well together while others will have great difficulty.

In this book, for ease of understanding, readiness levels are represented with a shape (triangle for above-grade level, square for on-grade level, and circle for below-grade level). In a classroom, however, a teacher might want to change the names for leveled groups from time to time. A teacher might use colors, animal names, or athletic team names to group students. For example, a teacher could cut out and distribute three different colors of construction paper squares, with each color representing a different readiness level. The teacher would tell all the "yellow square" students to find partners who also have a yellow square. This way, the teacher creates homogeneous groups while also allowing students to choose partners.

The following grouping strategies demonstrate various ways to group students in a differentiated classroom. This section is included so that you can learn to quickly group your students and easily apply the strategies.

Flexible Grouping

Flexible grouping means that members of a group change frequently. Routinely using the same grouping technique can lead to negative feelings, feelings of shame or a stigma associated with some group levels, lack of appropriate instruction, boredom, and behavior problems in the classroom. Flexible grouping can change the classroom environment daily, making it more interesting. It takes away the negative feelings and stigma of the struggling students because groups are always changing. No longer are the struggling students always in the same group.

Flexible grouping can occur within one lesson or over an entire unit. Try to modify groups from day to day, week to week, and unit to unit. Flexible grouping can include partner work, cooperative grouping, and whole-class grouping. Students' academic levels, interests, social chemistry, gender, or special needs can determine their placement in a particular group. Organize charts like the ones on the following pages to help you keep track of how you are grouping your students.

Grouping Students (cont.)

What Grouping Strategies Can I Use? (cont.)

Homogeneous Grouping

Homogeneous grouping brings together students who have the same readiness levels. It makes sense to group students homogeneously for reading groups and for language and mathematics skills lessons. To form groups, assess students' readiness levels in a content area. Then, order students from highest to lowest in readiness, and place them in order on a three-row horizontal grid.

One way to create homogeneous groups is by using the chart below. Notice that students in the same row have similar readiness levels.

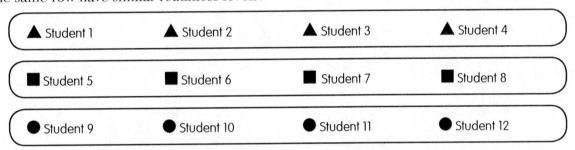

Homogeneous groups share similar readiness levels.

Heterogeneous Grouping

Heterogeneous grouping combines students with varied academic readiness levels. When grouping heterogeneously, look for some diversity in readiness and achievement levels so students can support one another as they learn together.

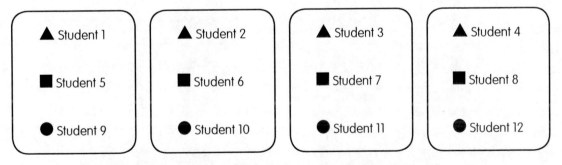

Heterogeneous groups have varying readiness levels.

Another strategy for heterogeneous grouping is to group by interest. Interest groups combine students with varied levels of achievement to create groups that have common interests. Other strategies for heterogeneous grouping include allowing students to self-select their groups, grouping by locality of seating arrangements in the classroom, and selecting groups at random.

Grouping Students *(cont.)*

What Grouping Strategies Can I Use? *(cont.)*

Flexogeneous Grouping

Flexogeneous grouping allows for the flexible grouping of homogeneous and heterogeneous groups within the same lesson. Students switch groups at least one time during the lesson to create another group. For example, the homogeneous groups meet for half the lesson and then switch to form heterogeneous groups for the rest of the lesson.

One easy flexogeneous grouping strategy is to jigsaw or mix up already established homogeneous groups. To jigsaw groups, allow homogeneous groups of students to work together for part of the lesson (circle, square, and triangle groups). Then, distinguish group members by labeling them *A*, *B*, and *C* within the same group. All the *As* form a new group, the *Bs* form a new group, and the *Cs* form a new group.

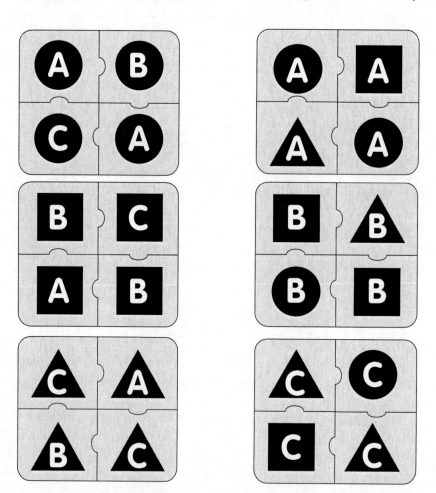

Flexogeneous grouping uses homogeneous and heterogeneous groups in a single lesson.

Working with English Language Learners

Strategies for Working with English Language Learners

Use visual media as an alternative to written responses. Have all students express their thinking through visual media, such as drawings, posters, or slide shows. This is an effective strategy for eliciting responses from English language learners. This also fosters creativity in all students, challenges above-grade-level students, provides opportunities for artistically inclined students who may struggle academically, and avoids singling out English language learners.

Frame questions to make the language accessible. At times, you will need to rephrase questions to clarify meaning for English language learners. Framing questions makes the language accessible to all students. Higher-order questions can be asked without reducing their rigor. Pose questions for English language learners with question stems or frames.

Example Question Stems/Frames

- What would happen if…?
- What is your opinion?
- Why do you think…?
- How would you prove…?
- Would it be better if…?

- How is _____ related to _____?
- If you could _____, what would you do?
- Can you invent _____?
- Why is _____ important?
- Why is _____ better than _____?

Give context to questions to enable understanding. This can be done by placing pictures or small icons directly next to key words. English language learners also benefit from chunking sentences. For example, with the question *In the ocean, how do wind and ocean currents make boats move?* English language learners can see right away that the question is about the ocean, so they have a context for answering the question.

Provide English language learners with sentence stems or frames to encourage higher-order thinking. These learners need language tools to help them express what they think. Sentence stems or frames will not only get the information you need and want from your English language learners, but it will also model how they should be speaking. You can provide these sentence stems or frames on small sticky notes for students to keep at their desks, or write them on laminated cards and distribute them to students when necessary.

Example Sentence Stems/Frames

- This is important because…
- This is better because…
- This is similar because…
- This is different because…

- I agree with _____ because…
- I disagree with _____ because…
- I think _____ because…
- I think _____ will happen because…

Partner up, and let partners share aloud. Have English language learners work with language-proficient students to answer questions, solve problems, or create projects. Language-proficient partners can provide the academic vocabulary needed to express ideas. Prepare your language-proficient students to work with language learners by explaining that they must speak slowly and clearly and give these learners time to think and speak.

Working with English Language Learners *(cont.)*

How Can I Support English Language Learners?

All teachers should know the language-acquisition level of each of their English language learners. Knowing these levels will help to plan instruction. Using visuals to support oral and written language for students at Level 1 will help make the language more comprehensible. Students at Levels 2 and 3 benefit from pair work in speaking tasks, but they will need additional individual support during writing and reading tasks. Students at Levels 4 and 5 may still struggle with comprehending the academic language used during instruction, as well as with reading and writing. Use the chart below to plan appropriate questions and activities.

Proficiency Levels for English Language Learners—Quick Glance

Proficiency Level	Questions to Ask	Activities/Actions		
Level 1—Entering • minimal comprehension • no verbal production	• Where is…? • What is the main idea? • What examples do you see? • What are the parts of…? • What would happen if…? • What is your opinion?	• listen • point	• draw • circle	• mime
Level 2—Beginning • limited comprehension • short spoken phrases	• Can you list three…? • What facts or ideas show…? • What do the facts mean? • How is _____ related to _____? • Can you invent…? • Would it be better if…?	• move • match	• select • choose	• act/act out
Level 3—Developing • increased comprehension • simple sentences	• How did _____ happen? • Which is your best answer? • What questions would you ask about…? • Why do you think…? • If you could _____, what would you do? • How would you prove…?	• name • label • tell/say	• list • categorize	• respond (with 1–2 words) • group
Level 4—Expanding • very good comprehension • some errors in speech	• How would you show…? • How would you summarize…? • What would result if…? • What is the relationship between…? • What is an alternative to…? • Why is this important?	• recall • compare/contrast • describe	• retell • explain • role-play	• define • summarize • restate
Level 5—Bridging • comprehension comparable to native English speakers • speaks using complex sentences	• How would you describe…? • What is meant by…? • How would you use…? • What ideas justify…? • What is an original way to show…? • Why is it better that…?	• analyze • evaluate • create	• defend • justify • express	• complete • support

How to Use This Book

Teacher Lesson Plans

Each lesson is presented in a straightforward, step-by-step format so that teachers can easily implement it right away.

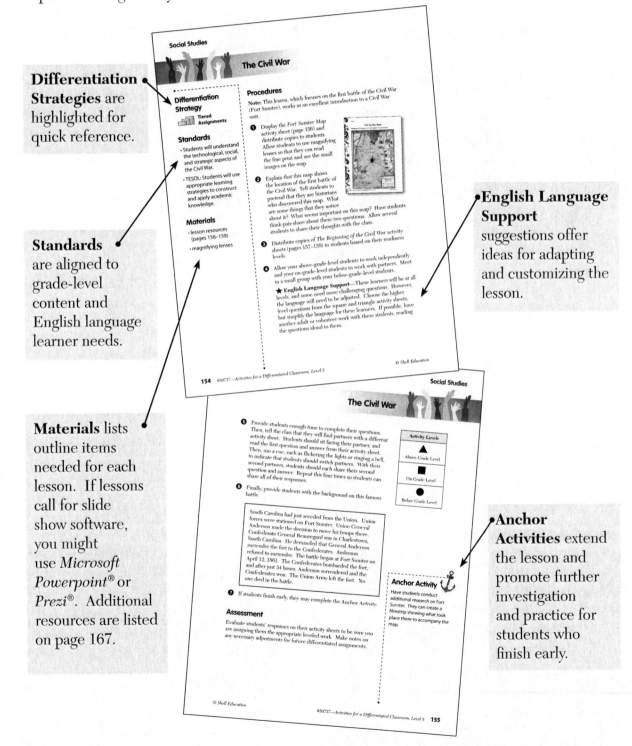

Differentiation Strategies are highlighted for quick reference.

Standards are aligned to grade-level content and English language learner needs.

Materials lists outline items needed for each lesson. If lessons call for slide show software, you might use *Microsoft Powerpoint®* or *Prezi®*. Additional resources are listed on page 167.

English Language Support suggestions offer ideas for adapting and customizing the lesson.

Anchor Activities extend the lesson and promote further investigation and practice for students who finish early.

How to Use This Book *(cont.)*

Lesson Resources

These pages include student reproducibles and teacher resources needed to implement each lesson.

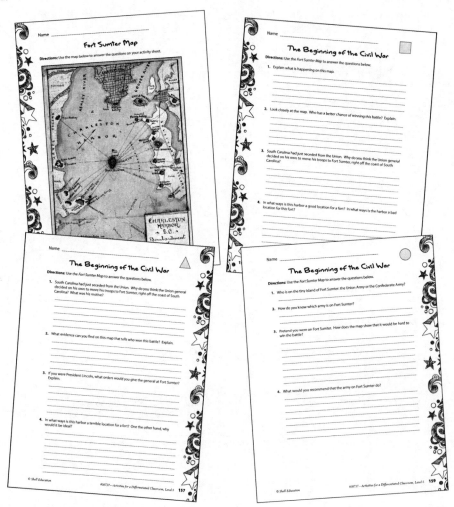

Teacher Resource CD

Helpful reproducibles and images are provided on the accompanying CD. Find a detailed listing of the CD contents on page 168.

- JPEGs of all photographs
- Reproducible PDFs of all student activity sheets and teacher resource pages
- Reproducible PDFs of blank graphic organizers
- Answer key

Correlations to Standards

Shell Education is committed to producing educational materials that are research and standards based. In this effort, we have correlated all of our products to the academic standards of all 50 states, the District of Columbia, and the Department of Defense Dependent Schools.

How to Find Standards Correlations

To print a customized correlation report of this product for your state, visit our website at **http://www.shelleducation.com** and follow the on-screen directions. If you require assistance in printing correlation reports, please contact Customer Service at 1-877-777-3450.

Purpose and Intent of Standards

The No Child Left Behind (NCLB) legislation mandates that all states adopt academic standards that identify the skills students will learn in kindergarten through grade 12. While many states had already adopted academic standards prior to NCLB, the legislation set requirements to ensure the standards were detailed and comprehensive.

Standards are designed to focus instruction and guide adoption of curricula. Standards are statements that describe the criteria necessary for students to meet specific academic goals. They define the knowledge, skills, and content students should acquire at each level. Standards are also used to develop standardized tests to evaluate students' academic progress.

Teachers are required to demonstrate how their lessons meet state standards. State standards are used in the development of all of our products, so educators can be assured that they meet the academic requirements of each state.

McREL Compendium

We use the Mid-continent Research for Education and Learning (McREL) Compendium to create standards correlations. Each year, McREL analyzes state standards and revises the compendium. By following this procedure, McREL is able to produce a general compilation of national standards. Each lesson in this product is based on one or more McREL standards. The chart on page 20 lists each standard taught in this book and the page numbers for the corresponding lessons.

TESOL Standards

The lessons in this book promote English language development for English language learners. The standards listed on page 21, from the Teachers of English to Speakers of Other Languages (TESOL) Association, support the language objectives presented throughout the lessons.

Correlations to Standards *(cont.)*

	McREL Standards	Lesson Title	Page
Language Arts	1.11, Level II: Students will write in response to literature.	Literature Response	40
	2.1, Level II: Students will use descriptive and precise language that clarifies and enhances ideas.	Writing with Details	28
	6.1, Level II: Students will use reading skills and strategies to understand a variety of literary passages and texts.	Identifying Genres	22
	7.5, Level II: Students will summarize and paraphrase information in texts.	Book in a Day	46
	1.10, Level III: Students will write persuasive compositions.	Persuasive Practice	34
	7.5, Level III: Students will draw conclusions and make inferences based on explicit and implicit information in texts.	Making Inferences	52
Mathematics	2.4, Level II: Students will understand the basic meaning of place value.	Number Sense	58
	2.5, Level II: Students will understand the relative magnitude and relationships among whole numbers, fractions, decimals, and mixed numbers.	Equivalent Fractions	70
	3.1, Level II: Students will multiply and divide whole numbers.	Long Division Algorithm	64
	4.1, Level II: Students will understand the basic measures of perimeter, area, volume, capacity, mass, angle, and circumference.	Exploring Volume	76
	5.0, Level II: Students will understand and apply basic and advanced properties of the concepts of geometry.	Geometry Wrap-Up	82
	8.3, Level II: Students will know that a variable is a letter or symbol that stands for one or more numbers.	Introducing Algebra	88
Science	2.3, Level II: Students will know that rock is composed of different combinations of minerals.	Rock Investigation	100
	4.1, Level II: Students will know that many characteristics of plants and animals are inherited from its parents, and other characteristics result from an individual's interactions with the environment.	Inherited Traits	112
	6.1, Level II: Students will know the organization of simple food chains and food webs.	Food Chains	106
	10.5, Level II: Students will know that when a force is applied to an object, the object either speeds up, slows down, or goes in a different direction.	Forces and Motion	124
	12.3, Level II: Students will plan and conduct simple investigations.	The Scientific Method	94
	7.1, Level III: Students will know basic ideas related to biological evolution.	Animal Adaptations	118
Social Studies	United States History, 5.1, Level II: Students will understand the factors that shaped the economic system in the American colonies.	Colonial America	130
	United States History, 6.3, Level II: Students will understand the major ideas in the Declaration of Independence, their sources, and how they became unifying ideas of American democracy.	Declaration of Independence	142
	United States History, 7.2, Level II: Students will understand the social, political, and economic effects of the American revolutionary victory on different groups.	Revolutionary Social Networking	136
	United States History, 10.6, Level II: Students will understand elements of early western migration.	Westward Expansion	148
	United States History, 14.1, Level II: Students will understand the technological, social, and strategic aspects of the Civil War.	The Civil War	154
	United States History, 15.1, Level II: Students will understand military, political, and social factors affecting the post-Civil War period.	Reconstruction	160

Correlations to Standards (cont.)

TESOL Standards		Lesson Title	Page
TESOL 2.2	Students will use English to obtain, process, construct, and provide subject matter information in spoken and written form to achieve academically in all content areas.	Identifying Genres	22
		Writing with Details	28
		Persuasive Practice	34
		Literature Response	40
		Book in a Day	46
		Making Inferences	52
		Long Division Algorithm	64
		Equivalent Fractions	70
		Exploring Volume	76
		Introducing Algebra	88
		Food Chains	106
		Forces and Motion	124
		Colonial America	130
		Revolutionary Social Networking	136
		Declaration of Independence	142
		Westward Expansion	148
TESOL 2.3	Students will use appropriate learning strategies to construct and apply academic knowledge.	Number Sense	58
		Geometry Wrap-Up	82
		The Scientific Method	94
		Rock Investigation	100
		Inherited Traits	112
		Animal Adaptations	118
		The Civil War	154
		Reconstruction	160

Identifying Genres

Differentiation Strategy

 Choices Board

Standards

- Students will use reading skills and strategies to understand a variety of literary passages and texts.

- TESOL: Students will use English to obtain, process, construct, and provide subject matter information in spoken and written form.

Materials

- lesson resources (pages 24–27)

- 30 or more books from all genres (*See page 167.*)

- index cards

- book bins

- construction paper

- art supplies

- pocket chart (*optional*)

- computer drawing software (*optional*)

Procedures

Preparation Note: Collect a wide variety of books from your classroom library or from the school library. Be sure to choose books from the following genres: *nonfiction, historical fiction, realistic fiction, science fiction, fantasy, biography/autobiography,* and *poetry.* Write each of these genre labels on an index card. Mix the books and place them in five bins. Each bin should have six to ten books representing different genres. Also, at the front of the room, lay seven sheets of construction paper, each in a different color, in a line on the floor.

❶ Place students in five heterogeneous groups. Explain to students that they will be book detectives. They will examine a group of books and organize them into categories. Explain that they will find clues about a book's category in the cover art, in the summary on the back cover, in chapter titles, and in the book's title. If necessary, they may even need to read a few pages of the first chapter to find out more. Give each group a book bin and ask students to begin sorting.

❷ Give students time to sort their books into categories of their own choice. In the end, there will be seven genre categories, but it is not necessary to identify seven categories in their bins yet. Call one group to the front of the room. Ask students to place each of their book categories on one of the colored pieces of construction paper. For example, they might place all the biographies/autobiographies on the green sheet of construction paper. Have group members explain the choices as they work.

❸ Call the next group to the front of the room. Have students look at the books that have already been placed. Ask them to place their books accordingly and to explain their choices. Continue this until all groups have had a chance to organize their books into categories. Discuss students' ideas and opinions about the exercise.

❹ Introduce students to the word *genre.* Tell students that genre is a word that means "category, class, or type," and is used to describe categories of books. Explain that genre is pronounced "ZHAWN-ruh." Practice the pronunciation together as a whole class.

Identifying Genres

5 Introduce students to the main genres that they will need to learn: *nonfiction, historical fiction, realistic fiction, science fiction, fantasy, biography/autobiography,* and *poetry.* There are other genres, but students should only focus on these for now. Distribute the index cards, labeled with the genres, to student volunteers. Ask the volunteers to place their genre labels on the book stacks that match them. If the book stacks do not match any of the labels, have the whole class work cooperatively to reorganize the books according to the genres on the labels.

★ **English Language Support**—Meet with these students in a small group to reinforce the defining characteristics of the seven genres. Provide examples in which the titles and cover art provide obvious clues about the topic. Create mini picture dictionaries of genres with these students. Each genre should have a graphic symbol to visually cue students about the types of books found in that category.

6 Distribute copies of the *Identifying Genres Choices Board* activity sheet (page 24) to students. Students should complete one on-level activity independently and a challenging activity with a friend. (For example, on-grade-level students would choose a square activity to complete independently and a triangle activity to complete with a friend.)

7 Another option is to display the leveled *Identifying Genres Choices Cards* activity sheets (pages 25–27) in a pocket chart. Have students choose activities from this display board. Provide students with any needed materials to help them complete the activities.

8 If students finish early, they may complete the Anchor Activity.

Assessment

Evaluate students' work to be sure that they understand the concepts that you have taught. If students complete their tasks with ease, you may need to adjust the level of activities to which they are assigned.

Anchor Activity

Have students choose a book from each genre that they would like to read this year. Ask them to write the titles and authors of these books on an index card. Then, have them draw up an agreement in which they promise to read seven books from seven different genres in a specific amount of time. Encourage students to design projects to demonstrate their comprehension of each book.

Name _____

Identifying Genres Choices Board

Directions: Choose two activities that match the shape assigned to you by your teacher.

Choose a nonfiction picture book, a fantasy picture book, and a historical fiction picture book to read. Then, create a three-way Venn diagram to compare the three genres. ▢	Choose any realistic fiction novel. Read the plot summary on the back cover. Rewrite the summary to turn the realistic fiction novel into a science fiction story. △	Choose a nonfiction picture book and a fiction picture book to read. Then, make a T-chart to compare the two genres. ◯
Choose two genres. Create two posters to advertise these genres. On each poster, include the genre name, a definition of the genre, and the titles of popular books that fit into the genre. ◯	Use computer software to design a logo for each of the seven genres. Choose fonts and graphics carefully so that others can recognize the genres at a glance. ▢	Create a mascot for each of the seven genres. Sketch a picture of each character in costume. Write a caption explaining your ideas. △
Think about your favorite genre. What do you like about the books in this genre? Write a poem that describes your favorite genre and explains your feelings about it. △	Which genre do you like best? Use a computer software program (or pencil and paper) to create a web about this genre. Include facts about the genre. Explain the things that you like about books in this category. ◯	What is your favorite genre? Write a persuasive essay to convince others to read a book from this genre. The essay body must state three reasons for your opinion and support each reason with three details. ▢
Make a genre brochure that libraries could give readers. It should list and describe the seven genres. You must also recommend three books from each genre. ▢	Broaden your horizons by choosing a book from a genre that you rarely read. Ask your teacher or a librarian for recommendations. Read the book and write an essay expressing your opinion of the genre. △	Give each genre a catchy new name that will make more readers want to check it out. Design seven simple signs to display the new names in the library. Each sign should give some basic facts about the genre. ◯

Name _____

Identifying Genres Choices Cards

Directions: Choose activities from the cards.

Choose any realistic fiction novel. Read the plot summary on the back cover. Rewrite the summary to turn the realistic fiction novel into a science fiction story.

Create a mascot for each of the seven genres. Sketch a picture of each character in costume. Write a caption explaining your ideas.

Think about your favorite genre. What do you like about the books in this genre? Write a poem that describes your favorite genre and explains your feelings about it.

Broaden your horizons by choosing a book from a genre that you rarely read. Ask your teacher or a librarian for recommendations. Read the book and write an essay expressing your opinion of the genre.

Identifying Genres Choices Cards

Directions: Choose activities from the cards.

Choose a nonfiction picture book, a fantasy picture book, and a historical fiction picture book to read. Then, create a three-way Venn diagram to compare the three genres.	Use computer software to design a logo for each of the seven genres. Choose fonts and graphics carefully so that others can recognize the genres at a glance.
What is your favorite genre? Write a persuasive essay to convince others to read a book from this genre. The essay body must state three reasons for your opinion and support each reason with three details.	Make a genre brochure that libraries could give readers. It should list and describe the seven genres. You must also recommend three books from each genre.

Name _____

Identifying Genres Choices Cards

Directions: Choose activities from the cards.

Choose a nonfiction picture book and a fiction picture book to read. Then, make a T-chart to compare the two genres.

Choose two genres. Create two posters to advertise these genres. On each poster, include the genre name, a definition of the genre, and the titles of popular books that fit into the genre.

Which genre do you like best? Use a computer software program (or pencil and paper) to create a web about this genre. Include facts about the genre. Explain the things that you like about books in this category.

Give each genre a catchy new name that will make more readers want to check it out. Design seven simple signs to display the new names in the library. Each sign should give some basic facts about the genre.

Writing with Details

Differentiation Strategy

 Tiered Graphic Organizers

Standards

- Students will use descriptive and precise language that clarifies and enhances ideas.

- TESOL: Students will use English to obtain, process, construct, and provide subject matter information in spoken and written form.

Materials

- lesson resources (pages 30–33)

Procedures

❶ Begin the lesson by reading this paragraph aloud:

> *The room was a mess. It was so dirty. "Yuck," said Sarah. "That is disgusting! We have to clean this junk up today."*

Ask students to describe the images that this paragraph formed in their minds. Begin by asking students what kind of room they pictured. Then, ask them what exactly made the mess—dirty dishes, piles of toys and games, smelly gym socks, or something else entirely. Tell students that the images in their minds, if there were any, varied greatly because the author *told* rather than *showed*.

❷ Read a second paragraph aloud. Ask students to close their eyes and prepare to listen carefully.

> *Megan's kitchen looked like a tornado had ripped through it. Two kitchen chairs lay toppled over on their sides. Sticky cookie dough dripped from the walls and the cabinets. Blue frosting and rainbow sprinkles decorated the countertops. A tower of mixing bowls and spoons teetered in the sink. Megan and her friend, Sarah, sat in the middle of the floor like rag dolls. They were exhausted after baking seven batches of cookies for the school bake sale!*

❸ Ask students to describe the images they saw in their minds after hearing the second paragraph. Explain to students that they were able to see these images because the author *showed* rather than *told* key details.

❹ Explain to students that there are several ways to show rather than tell. Ask students to point out techniques from the second paragraph. These include using specific words, using descriptions that incorporate the five senses, and using similes and metaphors. Explain each of these techniques and highlight examples from the passage.

Specific words: two chairs, frosting and rainbow sprinkles, mixing bowls and spoons, middle of the floor, seven batches.

Five-senses descriptions: sticky, blue, rainbow, teetered.

Similes and metaphors: like a tornado, tower of mixing bowls and spoons, like rag dolls.

Writing with Details

5 Distribute copies of the *Show, Don't Tell Warm-Up* activity sheet (page 30) to students. Read the first item aloud. Model for students how you would turn this into a showing example. Then, have students independently make changes to the other three examples. Circulate and assist as needed. Invite students to share their showing examples in class.

★ **English Language Support**—Instead of having English language learners work independently on the *Show, Don't Tell Warm-Up* activity sheets, bring them together into a small group. Conduct a shared writing activity in which all students contribute ideas for all four paragraph rewrites. Model your thinking and help students put their ideas into words.

6 Next, students will have opportunities to practice writing and recognizing showing details at their own readiness levels. Distribute copies of the *Show, Don't Tell Graphic Organizer* activity sheets (pages 31–33) to students based on their readiness levels. Have students with the triangle and square activity sheets read the directions and work independently to complete the organizers. Read the directions aloud to students with the circle sheets and English language learners.

7 If students finish early, they may complete the Anchor Activity.

Assessment

Evaluate students' graphic organizers to be sure that they understand the concepts. Additionally, students might share these organizers in small groups and complete peer assessments, stating whether they understand the concepts recorded in their classmates' graphic organizers.

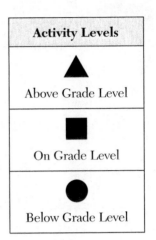

Activity Levels
▲
Above Grade Level
■
On Grade Level
●
Below Grade Level

Anchor Activity ⚓

Have students think of a person whom they know has a unique personality. This person could be a relative, a teacher, a friend, or a neighbor. Ask students to write a description of this person that makes readers feel like they have met him or her. Remind them to show, not tell!

Show, Don't Tell Warm-Up

Directions: Turn the telling examples below into showing examples.

1. The room was messy.

_____

_____

_____

_____

_____

_____

_____

2. He is very talented.

_____

_____

_____

_____

_____

_____

_____

3. Sam's sister is a pain.

_____

_____

_____

_____

_____

_____

4. The school lunch was gross.

_____

_____

_____

_____

_____

_____

Name _____

Show, Don't Tell Graphic Organizer

Part 1 Directions: On a separate sheet of paper, rewrite the *telling* example below as a *showing* paragraph. Use the three techniques taught in class to show rather than tell.

Our basement is spooky. I don't like to go down there by myself. It is very creepy.

Part 2 Directions: Identify the descriptive writing techniques you used in your writing and copy them onto the chart in the correct column. Some words and phrases might fit into more than one column.

Technique 1: _____	Technique 2: _____	Technique 3: _____

Part 3 Directions: Study the chart. Then, complete the self-evaluation below.

Criteria	Not at All	Somewhat	Very Well
1. I used all three techniques to improve the paragraph.	1	2	3
2. I can recognize all three techniques.	1	2	3
3. I can apply all three techniques effectively to my own writing.	1	2	3
4. I can write descriptions that show rather than tell.	1	2	3

Name _____

Show, Don't Tell Graphic Organizer

Part 1 Directions: On a separate sheet of paper, rewrite the *telling* example below as a *showing* paragraph. Use the three techniques taught in class to show rather than tell.

Our basement is spooky. I don't like to go down there by myself. It is very creepy.

Part 2 Directions: Identify the descriptive writing techniques you used in your writing and copy them onto the chart in the correct column. Some words and phrases might fit into more than one column.

Specific Words	Five-Senses Description	Similes and Metaphors

Part 3 Directions: Study the chart. What could you add to or change about your paragraph? Explain below.

_____

_____

_____

Name _____

Show, Don't Tell Graphic Organizer

Part 1 Directions: The description below does not *tell*—it *shows*. Read it carefully at least two times.

> *The basement in my house is spookier than a graveyard on Halloween night. The door creaks open with a ghostly screech. The stairway seems to tremble as I walk down into the darkness below. At the bottom of the stairs, I stop and peer into the deep shadows. Gray light slips in through a dirt-smeared window. In the far corner, the washing machine and dryer stand guard. I rush toward them with the heavy laundry basket. Out of the corner of my left eye, I see something small and quick dart across the floor. I hope it is not a mouse. I shove the dirty clothes into the washing machine, drop the basket, and turn toward the stairs. "Boo!" shouts my little brother, who is standing right behind me. "Eeeek!" I scream, and push him out of the way. I take the steps two at a time and slam the door behind me. Now we will see who is really scared. I hold the handle as my brother pounds on the door and begs me to open it.*

Part 2 Directions: Look for examples of the three descriptive writing techniques taught in class in the paragraph above. Copy the examples into the correct column of the chart. Some words and phrases might fit into more than one column. One example has been done for you.

Specific Words (the opposite of general words)	Five-Senses Descriptions (words that describe what you see, hear, smell, taste, or touch)	Similes and Metaphors (comparisons between two things that are unrelated)
		The basement in my house is spookier than a graveyard on Halloween night.

Persuasive Practice

Differentiation Strategy

 Menu of Options

Standards

- Students will write persuasive compositions.

- TESOL: Students will use English to obtain, process, construct, and provide subject matter information in spoken and written form.

Materials

- lesson resources (pages 36–39)
- chart paper and markers
- audio recorder
- slide show software
- newspapers

Procedures

1 Begin the lesson by asking students to think of one activity that they would really like to do that their parents do not normally allow. Invite volunteers to share their ideas, and list these on the board. Ideas may include watching a certain television show, staying up late, or visiting a particular place.

2 Tell students that they will have a chance to write a letter to their parents persuading their parents to allow them to do the activity. Explain that persuasion is the act of convincing someone to take action or to accept an idea.

3 Display the *Persuasive Essay Graphic Organizer* activity sheet (page 36). Choose one idea from the class list to use as the topic of a shared writing activity. (*Hint: It can be helpful if you choose a struggling student's topic to provide a jump start on the essay.*)

4 Work together as a whole class to craft a topic sentence. Explain that in a persuasive essay, the topic sentence should clearly state the writer's position or opinion. In this case, the topic sentence should state exactly what the writer wants. *I would like to stay up one hour later on Friday night.*

★ **English Language Support**—As you model how to write these parts of a persuasive essay, use different colored markers or chalk. For example, make the topic sentence red, the supporting sentences blue (or each a different color), and the concluding sentence black. Circle each part and label them to the side in the same color.

5 Ask students to support the topic sentence with three reasons. Explain that their reasons will be more effective if they try to see the subject from the audience's perspective. Ask the class to anticipate parents' possible objections to the example wish. Then, have students write at least one reason that refutes an objection. For example, *I know this is past my bedtime, but I would use the time to read a book.*

6 The most challenging part of essay writing for students is supporting their ideas. Often, students feel that if they have said it once, that should be enough. Model for students how to support each reason with three sentences that further explain the idea.

Persuasive Practice

7 Move on to the conclusion. Explain to students that this is the final chance to convince readers to accept their position. In the conclusion, students should restate the main idea, summarize supporting arguments, and give a powerful and motivating statement.

8 Return to the introduction. Work together to write a lead or hook that will draw readers into the essay. This comes before the topic sentence and should be creative and attention-catching. It should flow well with the topic sentence.

9 Read the essay aloud from start to finish. Ask students if they want to add or change anything. Display the shared writing in the classroom for students to use as a reference while writing their own persuasive letters.

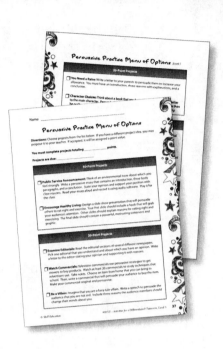

10 Distribute copies of the *Persuasive Practice Menu of Options* activity sheets (pages 37–38) to students. Explain to students that they will choose activities from the menu (or propose their own projects) to practice more persuasive writing. Decide ahead of time how many points students need to complete from the menu. Review the choices with students, and answer any questions about the activities.

11 Distribute copies of the *Persuasive Practice Action Plan* activity sheet (page 39) to students. Have students complete it to prepare for their writing activities.

12 Distribute copies of the *Persuasive Essay Graphic Organizer* activity sheet (page 36) for students to use to plan their menu of options activities. Provide students with any needed materials to help them complete the activities. Give students time to complete the assignments. Allow students to choose one project to share with the class.

13 If students finish early, they may complete the Anchor Activity.

Assessment

Evaluate the menu of options tasks to be sure that the lesson objectives have been met. Prepare to reteach concepts to small groups of students.

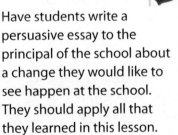

Anchor Activity

Have students write a persuasive essay to the principal of the school about a change they would like to see happen at the school. They should apply all that they learned in this lesson.

Name _____

Persuasive Essay Graphic Organizer

Directions: Use the graphic organizer to help you write your persuasive essay.

Introduction

Hook: _____

_____

Topic Sentence: _____

_____

Body

Reason 1:_____

_____

Support 1:_____

_____

Support 2:_____

_____

Support 3:_____

_____

Reason 2:_____

_____

Support 1:_____

_____

Support 2:_____

_____

Support 3:_____

_____

Reason 3:_____

_____

Support 1:_____

_____

Support 2:_____

_____

Support 3:_____

_____

Conclusion

Main idea: _____

_____

Summary of reasons: _____

_____

Powerful statement: _____

_____

Name _____

Persuasive Practice Menu of Options

Directions: Choose projects from the list below. If you have a different project idea, you may propose it to your teacher. If accepted, it will be assigned a point value.

You must complete projects totaling _____ points.

Projects are due: _____

50-Point Projects

☐ **Public Service Announcement:** Think of an environmental issue about which you feel strongly. Write a persuasive essay that contains an introduction, three body paragraphs, and a conclusion. State your opinion and support your position with clear reasons. Read your essay aloud and record it using audio software. Play it for the class.

☐ **Encourage Healthy Living:** Design a slide show presentation that will persuade others to eat right and exercise. Your first slide should include a hook that will grab your audience's attention. Other slides should explain reasons for eating right and exercising. The final slide should contain a powerful, motivating statement and graphic.

30-Point Projects

☐ **Examine Editorials:** Read the editorial sections of several different newspapers. Pick one editorial that you understand and about which you have an opinion. Write a letter to the editor stating your opinion and supporting it with reasons.

☐ **Watch Commercials:** Television commercials use persuasive strategies to get viewers to buy products. Watch at least 20 commercials to study techniques that advertisers use. Take notes. Choose an item from home that you can bring to school. Then, write a commercial that will persuade your audience to buy the item. Make your commercial original and persuasive.

☐ **Be a Villain:** Imagine that you are a fairy-tale villain. Write a speech to persuade the audience that you are not evil. Include three reasons the audience members should change their minds about you.

Persuasive Practice Menu of Options *(cont.)*

20-Point Projects

☐ **You Need a Raise:** Write a letter to your parents to persuade them to increase your allowance. You must have an introduction, three reasons with explanations, and a conclusion.

☐ **Character Choices:** Think about a book that you have recently read. Write a letter to the main character. Persuade the main character to make a different choice than he or she made in the book. Include three reasons and explain each one clearly.

10-Point Projects

☐ **Fact vs. Opinion:** Write a paragraph that explains the difference between fact and opinion. Explain why people often confuse these when they feel strongly about something.

☐ **Personal Persuasion:** Think of a time when someone persuaded you to do something. Write a paragraph about the experience. Include your ideas about what made that person so persuasive.

☐ **Professional Persuaders:** Make a list of 15 careers in which workers use persuasion.

Student-Proposed Projects

☐ _____

_____

_____

☐ _____

_____

_____

Name _____

Persuasive Practice Action Plan

Directions: Complete an action plan to help plan your projects.

You must complete projects totaling _____ points.

Projects are due: _____

Projects	Points Possible	Steps to Take
Total Points:		

Literature Response

Differentiation Strategy

 Bloom's Taxonomy

Standards

- Students will write in response to literature.

- TESOL: Students will use English to obtain, process, construct, and provide subject matter information in spoken and written form.

Materials

- lesson resources (pages 42–45)

- five or six nonfiction articles with text features

Procedures

❶ Distribute copies of the same high-interest nonfiction article to each student. Have students partner with a classmate nearby for a think-pair-share activity. Ask them to look at the article and to think about the features that make it different from a novel or a picture book. Have students point out these features to their partners. Then, invite pairs to share their ideas with the class.

❷ Make sure to point out and explain the use of bold print, italics, graphics, titles, headings, and captions. Explain that these features are designed to help readers navigate nonfiction texts more easily. Tell students that a pre-reading strategy you would like them to use is to scan text features before beginning a nonfiction reading assignment.

★ **English Language Support**—Display the terms *bold print, italics, graphics, titles, headings,* and *captions* with simple definitions and examples in the classroom for these students to use as references throughout the lesson.

❸ Read the article aloud and discuss it as a class. Ask students to identify the main idea of the article. Have them identify the topic sentence of each paragraph. Also, ask them to identify the purpose of the article. Work together as a whole class to summarize the content. Then, ask students to share their opinions or to evaluate the article.

❹ Explain to students that the ability to read, understand, and evaluate a nonfiction article is an important skill. Tell them that an article review has two basic parts—the summary and the evaluation. Students will have a chance to practice both of these skills when they complete the leveled questions.

Literature Response

5 Distribute copies of the *Literature Response Questions* activity sheets (pages 42–44) to students based on their readiness levels. Then, meet with each group separately, beginning with the circle group, to explain the assignment and answer students' questions.

6 Invite students to choose a nonfiction article from the selections that you have provided. Have them read the article and complete the leveled questions based on Bloom's Taxonomy.

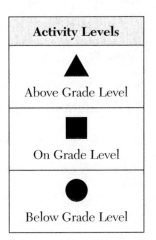

Activity Levels	
▲	Above Grade Level
■	On Grade Level
●	Below Grade Level

7 If students finish early, they may complete the Anchor Activity.

Assessment

Use the *Literature Response Rubric* (page 45) to assess students' responses. To use the rubric, read the descriptions in each row. Choose the description that best matches the student's work and circle it. To get the total score, multiply the number above the box you circled with the tens digit of the percent for that row. For example, if you circled the description under 7 in the *summarizing* row of the rubric, you would multiply 7 x 4 = 28. That is the score for that row. Do this for each row. Then add the scores together to get a number out of 100 possible points.

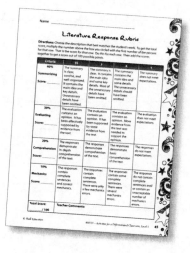

Anchor Activity ⚓

Have students write responses to genres of literature other than nonfiction texts. Students should summarize the main idea and details. Encourage students to share their responses with their classmates.

Name _____

Literature Response Questions

Directions: Respond to all of the questions using complete sentences.

Title of Article: _____

Author: _____

Evaluating: What is your opinion about this article? Explain.

_____

_____

_____

_____

_____

Creating: If you had to show another viewpoint related to this article, what would that viewpoint be? Explain this new point of view in the space below. Be creative.

_____

_____

_____

_____

_____

Analyzing: In the space below, create a graphic organizer to compare and contrast this article with the article that you read in class. For this comparison, the content of the articles is not the focus. Instead, focus on the text features and the format of the articles.

_____

_____

_____

_____

_____

_____

_____

_____

Name _____

Literature Response Questions

Directions: Respond to all of the questions using complete sentences.

Title of Article: _____

Author: _____

Understanding: What is the article about? Write a short summary on the lines below. Be sure to include the main idea and important details.

_____

_____

_____

_____

_____

_____

Analyzing: Why would an article about this topic need to be written? Explain.

_____

_____

_____

_____

_____

Evaluating: What is your opinion about this article? Explain it.

_____

_____

_____

_____

_____

_____

_____

_____

Name _____

Literature Response Questions

Directions: Respond to the questions using complete sentences.

Title of Article: _____

Author: _____

Remembering: Complete the graphic organizer with information from the article.

Main Idea

Supporting Detail

Supporting Detail

Supporting Detail

Understanding: If a friend asked you what the article was about, what would you say?

_____
_____
_____
_____
_____

Evaluating: Did you like the article? Explain why or why not.

_____
_____
_____
_____
_____

Name _____

Literature Response Rubric

Directions: Choose the description that best matches the student's work. To get the total score, multiply the number above the box you circled with the first number of the percent for that row. That is the score for that row. Do this for each row. Then add the scores together to get a score out of 100 possible points.

Criteria	10	7	4	1
40% **Summarizing** Score: _____	The summary is clear, concise, and well-organized. It contains the main idea and key details. Unnecessary details have been omitted.	The summary is clear. It contains the main idea and some key details. Most of the unnecessary details have been omitted.	The summary contains the main idea and some details. The unnecessary details should have been omitted.	The summary does not meet expectations.
30% **Evaluating** Score: _____	The evaluation contains an opinion. It has been effectively supported by evidence from the text.	The evaluation contains an opinion. It has been supported by some evidence from the text.	The evaluation contains an opinion. More evidence from the text was needed to support the opinion.	The evaluation does not meet expectations.
20% **Comprehension** Score: _____	The responses demonstrate in-depth comprehension of the text.	The responses demonstrate comprehension of the text.	The responses demonstrate basic comprehension of the text.	The responses do not meet expectations.
10% **Mechanics** Score: _____	The responses contain complete sentences and correct mechanics.	The responses contain complete sentences. There were only a few mechanics errors.	The responses contain some complete sentences. There were several mechanics errors.	The responses do not contain complete sentences and/or contain an unacceptable number of mechanics errors.
Total Score: _____ / 100	**Teacher Comments:**			

Book in a Day

Differentiation Strategy

 Tiered Assignments

Standards

- Students will summarize and paraphrase information in texts.

- TESOL: Students will use English to obtain, process, construct, and provide subject matter information in spoken and written form.

Materials

- lesson resources, (pages 48–51)

- novel, one to two grade levels below the average reading level of your students

- stapler

Procedures

Preparation Note: Purchase several copies of a used or paperback novel that is one or two grade levels below the average reading level of your students. Carefully break apart the books and section them off by chapters. Staple each chapter together, but keep them separate from other chapters. Make at least one complete set of all the chapters stapled into booklet form. If you have additional copies of the book, you may want to make two or three sets.

1 Show the class a complete, intact version of the book. Explain that today the class will read this entire book! Tell them not to be nervous. Explain that you will help them by reading the first chapter aloud.

2 Read the first chapter aloud. Pause and ask questions. Discuss the main character or characters, the setting, and the events in the first chapter.

3 Tell students that they will be reading the rest of the book today. Then, show them how you have sectioned off the book. Explain that each student will read one chapter of the book. Each student will become an expert on his or her own chapter. Then, each student will complete an activity about his or her reading to share with the class. At the end of the presentations, students will all feel as if they have read the entire book. In fact, the class will have read the book in one day.

4 Choose carefully when assigning chapters to students. Assign long, complicated chapters to strong readers. Assign short, straightforward chapters to struggling readers.

★ **English Language Support**—Pair these students with on-grade-level students. Ask the on-grade-level students to read the chapter aloud slowly and carefully. Have them summarize the events orally for their partners.

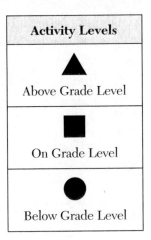

Book in a Day

❺ After students have read their assigned chapters, distribute copies of the *Book in a Day* activity sheets (pages 48–50) to students based on their readiness levels.

Activity Levels
▲
Above Grade Level
■
On Grade Level
●
Below Grade Level

❻ Allow time for students to complete their activity sheets and present their chapters to the class.

❼ If students finish early, they may complete the Anchor Activity.

Assessment

Use the *Book in a Day Rubric* (page 51) to assess student work.

Anchor Activity

Have students read other chapters of the book to see how quickly they can read the book. Ask them to make notes about key events in each chapter on a sticky note and post it at the end of the chapter. Explain that they are acting as fact checkers for their peers' assignments.

Name _____

Book in a Day

Directions: Read the chapter carefully. You are the class expert on this part of the story. Then, complete the sheet to share what you read with your classmates.

1. Chapter: _____

2. Main Characters: _____

_____

3. Settings: _____

_____

4. Make notes here that summarize the chapter. Include only the most important details.

_____

_____

_____

_____

_____

5. Do you think that the characters are believable? Why or why not?

_____

_____

_____

_____

6. Think of at least three questions that you have about the book based on this chapter. List them below.

_____

_____

_____

_____

7. Predict what will happen next in the story. Explain your prediction.

_____

_____

_____

_____

Name _____

Book in a Day

Directions: Read the chapter carefully. You are the class expert on this part of the story. Then, complete the sheet to share what you read with your classmates.

1. Chapter: _____

2. Main Characters: _____

   _____

3. Settings: _____

   _____

4. Summarize the chapter. Include only the most important details.

   _____

   _____

   _____

   _____

   _____

   _____

   _____

5. Make a connection between this story and another story or your own life. Explain the connection.

   _____

   _____

   _____

   _____

   _____

6. Predict what will happen next in the story. Explain your prediction.

   _____

   _____

   _____

   _____

   _____

   _____

Name _____

Book in a Day

Directions: Read the chapter carefully. You are the class expert on this part of the story. Then, complete the sheet to share what you read with your classmates.

1. Chapter: _____

2. Main Characters: _____

_____

3. Settings: _____

_____

4. Sketch three pictures from the chapter. Sketch an event from the beginning, an event from the middle, and an event from the end of your chapter. Make sure you include the most important events.

Beginning	**Middle**	**End**

5. Predict what will happen next in the story. Explain your prediction.

_____

_____

_____

_____

Name _____

Book in a Day Rubric

Reading the Rubric: Your project has been graded on four criteria. You earned a score from 1 to 5 for each item. Your project is worth a total of 20 points.

Criteria	Poor	Needs Work	Fair	Strong	Outstanding
You read the assigned chapter.	1	2	3	4	5
Your summary is complete and accurate.	1	2	3	4	5
Your summary demonstrates strong comprehension of the text.	1	2	3	4	5
Your responses are thoughtful.	1	2	3	4	5

Score: _____ /20

Teacher Comments: _____

_____

- -

Name _____

Book in a Day Rubric

Reading the Rubric: Your project has been graded on four criteria. You earned a score from 1 to 5 for each item. Your project is worth a total of 20 points.

Criteria	Poor	Needs Work	Fair	Strong	Outstanding
You read the assigned chapter.	1	2	3	4	5
Your summary is complete and accurate.	1	2	3	4	5
Your summary demonstrates strong comprehension of the text.	1	2	3	4	5
Your responses are thoughtful.	1	2	3	4	5

Score: _____ /20

Teacher Comments: _____

_____

Making Inferences

Differentiation Strategy

 Leveled Learning Contracts

Standards

• Students will draw conclusions and make inferences based on explicit and implicit information in texts.

• TESOL: Students will use English to obtain, process, construct, and provide subject matter information in spoken and written form.

Materials

• lesson resources (pages 54–57)

• clip from a popular movie (*See page 167.*)

• passage from a novel

• sticky notes

Procedures

1 Find out what students know about informational texts by doing a quick informal evaluation. This can be done by asking students to define the term *inference* and by asking questions about how and why inferences are made.

2 Evaluate student answers and assign them to the appropriate *Making Inferences Learning Contract* activity sheet (pages 54–56). Students who answer all questions correctly receive the triangle contract. Students who miss one or two questions receive the square contract. Students who miss more than two questions receive the circle contract.

3 For each student, mark the *Making Inferences Learning Contract Outline* activity sheet (page 57) to indicate which activities must be completed. Attach the appropriate learning contract to the outline. Distribute these packets to students. Review the outlines and contracts with the class and answer their questions. Visit students individually to sign their contracts. Provide students with any needed materials to help them complete the activities.

4 If students finish their contracts early, they may complete the Anchor Activity.

Part 1—Introduction to Inferences

1 The first lesson will introduce the skill of making inferences, using the familiar medium of popular movies. Ahead of time, choose a scene from a popular movie in which viewers can enhance their understanding through inferences.

2 Play the movie clip all the way through. Next, prompt students with a guiding question about the scene that requires students to make an inference. (*What kind of person is the character? What is his/her motive in this scene? What does he/she really believe?*) Play the clip again and ask students to share their answers to the question.

Making Inferences

❸ Play the clip a third time and pause the movie. Help students break down their inferences. Explain that an inference is made by combining what you see, hear, or read with what you already know. Walk them through this thought process as it relates to the movie clip. For example, if a character stomps up the stairs and slams her bedroom door, you can infer that she is angry.

❹ Read a passage aloud from a novel. Have students use the same process to make inferences about the text. Ask them to write down two inferences using this format:
What I read + What I already know = My inference

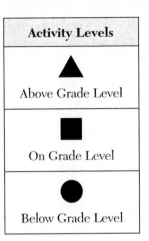

Activity Levels
▲
Above Grade Level
■
On Grade Level
●
Below Grade Level

Part 2—Making Inferences Practice

❶ Students with square contracts may begin working on their activities independently. Provide students with a reading passage slightly below the average independent reading level of the group. Have students read the passage independently. Then, read the passage aloud to students. Invite them to share inferences with the group. Each time, ask them to format their answers this way:
What I read + What I already know = My inference

Part 3—More Practice Making Inferences

❶ Students with the circle contracts will join you for the review activity. Students with square and triangle contracts will continue working independently.

❷ Help students with circle contracts get started on their learning contract activities. The whole class should be working on the activities during this time.

★ **English Language Support**—Meet with these students in a small group. Help them choose appropriate activities and modify them to meet individual needs.

Assessment

Use the *Making Inferences Learning Contract Rubric* (page 57) to assess student work. Continue to model and discuss the skill of making inferences at every opportunity.

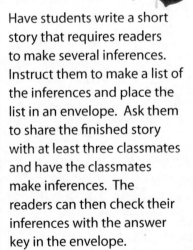

Anchor Activity

Have students write a short story that requires readers to make several inferences. Instruct them to make a list of the inferences and place the list in an envelope. Ask them to share the finished story with at least three classmates and have the classmates make inferences. The readers can then check their inferences with the answer key in the envelope.

Name _____

Making Inferences Learning Contract

Directions: Read the activity choices below. Choose two activities to complete. Fill out the contract with your choices.

1. Study the photograph of the quarter. Make at least five inferences about the coin and the subject on the coin. Write each inference in this format:
   What I see + What I already know = My inference

2. You can make inferences anywhere! As you go about your daily life, pay careful attention to the people around you. Listen to kids in the lunchroom, watch your teammates at practice, and study your family members at home. Use what you see and hear plus what you already know to make five inferences. Sketch the scene of each inference in cartoon form. Add dialogue, thought bubbles, and an explanation below each sketch.

3. Write the script for a three-act mystery play. Make sure you do not give all the details away in the dialogue. Ask classmates to practice with you and perform the play for an audience. Have the audience make a list of inferences as they watch. Invite them to share their inferences after the play.

4. There are many types of inferences. Research the different types. Then, find an example of at least 10 types of inferences in the book you are currently reading and in books you have recently read. Make a chart with the inference, an explanation of how you made it, and the type of inference you made.

I, _____, will complete activities

_____ and _____.

Project due date: _____.

Student signature: _____

Teacher signature: _____

Name _____

Making Inferences Learning Contract

Directions: Read the activity choices below. Choose two activities to complete. Fill out the contract with your choices.

1. Study the engraving of George Washington at Valley Forge. Make at least five inferences about the scene. Write each inference in this format:
    What I see + What I already know = My inference

2. Think about someone you know well, such as a family member or a close friend. List three character traits of that person. Some examples of character traits are loyalty, generosity, bravery, kindness, and friendliness. Then, think of the real-life events that helped you to make those character inferences. Work backward to describe the evidence that led you to draw your conclusions.

3. Write a personal narrative about something surprising or exciting that happened to you. Do not give away all the facts of your story. Hide details in clues that require the reader to make inferences. Your essay should have at least three paragraphs.

4. There are many types of inferences. Character inferences, setting inferences, vocabulary inferences, and relationship inferences are four common types. Find an example of each of these four types of inferences in the book you are currently reading or in books you have recently read. Make a chart with the inference, an explanation of how you made it, and the type of inference you made.

I, _____, will complete activities

_____ and _____.

Project due date: _____.

Student signature: _____

Teacher signature: _____

Name _____

Making Inferences Learning Contract

Directions: Read the activity choices below. Choose at least one activity to complete. Fill out the contract with your choices.

1. Study the beach photograph. Make inferences to answer the following questions:

    - *What is the relationship between the three people in the photograph?*

    - *Where might this photograph have been taken?*

    - *Why was this photograph taken?*

    - *What is going on in this picture?*

    - *What emotions are the people in the picture feeling?*

    - Write each inference in this format:
    What I see + What I already know = My inference

2. Think about someone you know well, such as a family member or a close friend. Name one character trait that person has. Some examples of character traits are loyalty, generosity, bravery, kindness, and friendliness. Then, think about how that person has shown that character trait. *Did your loyal best friend defend you when she heard classmates gossiping?* Write a paragraph about the real-life event or events that helped you see your subject's true character.

3. Character inferences are inferences you make to describe character traits. In the book you are reading now or in a book you have recently read, make three character inferences. Mark the pages where you made inferences with sticky notes. On each sticky note, write the inference in this format:
What I read + What I already know = My inference.

4. Vocabulary inferences are inferences you make to figure out the meaning of new words. The word itself, root words, prefixes and suffixes, and the context give clues about the word's meaning. In the book you are reading now or in a book you have recently read, make three vocabulary inferences. Mark the pages where you made inferences with sticky notes. On each sticky note, write the inference in this format:
What I read + What I already know = My inference.

I, _____, will complete activities

_____ and _____.

Project due date: _____.

Student signature: _____

Teacher signature: _____

© *Shell Education*

Name _____

Making Inferences Learning Contract Outline

Directions: You are required to participate in the activities that are checked below. If you do not see a check by an activity, you can use that time to work on the activities you have chosen on your Making Inferences Learning Contract.

Part 1—Introduction to Inferences	Part 2—Making Inferences Practice
☐ large-group instruction ☐ homework assignment	☐ large-group review ☐ small-group instruction ☐ homework assignment
Part 3—More Practice Making Inferences ☐ small-group review	**Learning Contract** ☐ learning contract activities

– –

Name _____

Making Inferences Learning Contract Rubric

Reading the Rubric: Your project has been graded on five criteria. You earned a score from 1 to 5 for each item. Your project is worth a total of 25 points.

Criteria	Poor	Needs Work	Fair	Strong	Outstanding
You followed the activity guidelines.	1	2	3	4	5
You used the text plus background knowledge to make inferences.	1	2	3	4	5
You demonstrated understanding of different types of inferences.	1	2	3	4	5
Your inferences deepened your comprehension.	1	2	3	4	5
You proofread your responses so there are few errors.	1	2	3	4	5

Score: _____ / 25

Teacher Comments: _____

_____

Number Sense

Differentiation Strategy

 Choices Board

Standards

- Students will understand the basic meaning of place value.
- TESOL: Students will use appropriate learning strategies to construct and apply academic knowledge.

Materials

- lesson resources (pages 60–63)
- large and individual place value charts
- index cards
- pocket chart

Procedures

★ **English Language Support**—Before teaching the lesson, give these students and students working below grade level a small place value chart to have at their desks. Review the name of each place on the chart. Then guide the group in pronouncing several large numbers. This will help prepare students for the *Mystery Number* game.

❶ Display a large place value chart where all students can clearly see it. Then, tell students that they will play a guessing game called *Mystery Number*. Invite students to each choose a partner for the game. Make sure each pair has scrap paper.

❷ Give the clues for the first mystery number aloud and write them on the board.

The mystery number has five digits.

There is a 3 in the ten thousands place.

None of the other digits is a 3.

The mystery number is the smallest possible number these five digits can make.

(answer: 30,000)

❸ Have students share their answers and explain their thinking. Then, give clues for another mystery number:

The mystery number has four digits.

There is a 7 in the hundreds place.

There is a 5 in the ones place.

The digit in the tens place is the difference between 7 and 5.

The number is less than 2,000.

(answer: 1,725)

❹ Tell students that they will now write their own riddles for the *Mystery Number* game. Explain that their mystery numbers can have between one and six digits. Ask them not to use decimals at this time. Have students write at least four clues for each mystery number. They must make sure that their clues narrow down the possibilities so that there is only one possible answer.

5 Students will write clues for five different mystery numbers. Distribute five index cards to each pair. Instruct students to put their names on the backs of the cards and number the cards one through five. Students should write clues for the mystery number on the front. Have them make answer keys on separate sheets of paper and turn them in to you.

6 Collect students' *Mystery Number* riddles and use them throughout the year to play *Mystery Number* as a whole class. Other options include having students trade cards and play the game independently, or placing the cards at a learning center.

7 Assign a shape to students based on their readiness levels. Display the leveled *Number Sense Choices Cards* activity sheets (pages 61–63) in a pocket chart. Tell students they will choose at least two activities that match the shape you assigned them. Read the choices aloud and answer students' questions.

8 Distribute copies of the *Number Sense Choices Board* activity sheet (page 60) so that each student has a copy of the activities as they work. Explain to students that these are challenging problems that will require them to use problem-solving strategies, such as guess-and-check, work backwards, make a list, and draw a picture.

9 If students finish early, they may complete the Anchor Activity.

Assessment

Evaluate students' work on the choices board to be sure that they are working at the appropriate levels and understand the concepts that have been taught.

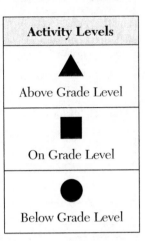

Activity Levels
▲
Above Grade Level
■
On Grade Level
●
Below Grade Level

Anchor Activity

Have students make up three new number sense problems to add to the choices board.

Name _____

Number Sense Choices Board

Directions: Choose two activities that match the shape assigned by your teacher.

You can add the digits in 987,654,321 to get a sum of 99. To do this, how many addition signs should be put between the digits, and where must you put them? ◻	Find the Mystery Number. It has a 1 in the thousands place. The digit in the tens place is 9 times the digit in the thousands place. The digit in the ones place is a hand without a thumb. The digit in the hundreds place is 2 less than the number in the tens. △	A man has to be at work at 9:00 A.M. It takes him 15 minutes to get dressed, 20 minutes to eat, and 35 minutes to walk to work. How long does he need to get to work on time? Write your answer in hours. ◯
Rachel opened her math book. The sum of the page numbers on the facing pages was 243. To which pages did she open her book? ◯	Place the digits 9, 4, 7, 6, 5, and 1 in the boxes to get the largest result. Use each digit only once. ◻◻ x ◻◻ + ◻ x ◻ = ? ◻	Find the answers to these questions: How many odd three-digit numbers have digits that add together to equal 5? How many even three-digit numbers are greater than 700, with digit totals of 11? Explain your problem-solving steps. △
A traffic light at one intersection changes every 32 seconds. The light at the next intersection changes every 28 seconds. How long will it take for them to change at the same time? △	Use any digits between 1 and 9 only once in each box. The answer to the equation should always be 9. How many different equations can you make? ◻ + ◻ x ◻ = 9 ◯	A farmer has chickens and cows on his farm. There are 78 legs and 27 heads in all. How many chickens and how many cows does the farmer have? Explain your thinking. ◻
Using real grocery store prices, prepare a grocery list of 10 items that will cost between $26 and $28. You may not go under or over the price range. You may not buy more than two of the same item. ◯	Using real grocery store prices, prepare a grocery list of 15 items that will cost between $29.50 and $32.75. You may not go under or over the price range. You may not buy more than two of the same item. ◻	Using real grocery store prices, prepare a grocery list of 25 items that will cost between $38.75 and $41.25. You may not go under or over the price range. You may not buy more than one of the same item. △

Number Sense Choices Cards

Directions: Choose any two activities from the cards below.

Find the Mystery Number.

It has a 1 in the thousands place.

The digit in the tens place is 9 times the digit in the thousands place.

The digit in the ones place is a hand without a thumb.

The digit in the hundreds place is 2 less than the number in the tens.

Find the answers to these questions: How many odd three-digit numbers have digits that add together to equal 5?

How many even three-digit numbers are greater than 700, with digit totals of 11?

Explain your problem-solving steps.

A traffic light at one intersection changes every 32 seconds.

The light at the next intersection changes every 28 seconds.

How long will it take for them to change at the same time?

Using real grocery store prices, prepare a grocery list of 25 items that will cost between $38.75 and $41.25.

You may not go under or over the price range.

You may not buy more than one of the same item.

Name _____

Number Sense Choices Cards

Directions: Choose any two activities from the cards below.

You can add the digits in 987,654,321 to get a sum of 99.

To do this, how many addition signs should be put between the digits, and where must you put them?

Place the digits 9, 4, 7, 6, 5, and 1 in the boxes to get the largest result. Use each digit only once.

□□ x □□ + □ x □ = ?

A farmer has chickens and cows on his farm.

There are 78 legs and 27 heads in all.

How many chickens and how many cows does the farmer have?

Explain your thinking.

Using real grocery store prices, prepare a grocery list of 15 items that will cost between $29.50 and $32.75.

You may not go under or over the price range.

You may not buy more than two of the same item.

Number Sense Choices Cards

Directions: Choose any two activities from the cards below.

A man has to be at work at 9:00 A.M.

It takes him 15 minutes to get dressed, 20 minutes to eat, and 35 minutes to walk to work.

How long does he need to get to work on time?

Write your answer in hours.

Rachel opened her math book. The sum of the page numbers on the facing pages was 243.

To which pages did she open her book?

Use any digits between 1 and 9 only once in each box. The answer to the equation should always be 9.

How many different equations can you make?

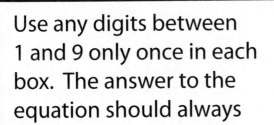

$$\square + \square \times \square = 9$$

Using real grocery store prices, prepare a grocery list of 10 items that will cost between $26.00 and $28.00.

You may not go under or over the price range.

You may not buy more than two of the same item.

Long Division Algorithm

Differentiation Strategy

 Leveled Learning Contracts

Standards

- Students will multiply and divide whole numbers.

- TESOL: Students will use English to obtain, process, construct, and provide subject matter information in spoken and written form.

Materials

- lesson resources (pages 66–69)

- large, unopened package of snacks

- audio recorder

- manipulatives

- sample division problems

- Internet

- number cubes

- index cards

- plastic storage bags

Procedures

1 Find out what students know about division by posing a real-world problem for students to solve. Present an unopened package of snacks, such as cookies or crackers. Tell students that you brought these to share with the whole class. (Be aware of any food allergies your students may have.) Ask students how you can make this fair for everyone. Allow them to work cooperatively to problem-solve.

2 When the students have reached a fair and logical conclusion, distribute the snacks according to the plan. As students snack, ask them to share their observations about the problem-solving process. Use this discussion to informally evaluate students' understanding of division concepts.

3 Find out which students can use the division algorithm. Write a long-division problem on the board. Ask students to solve the problem independently. Walk around the room with a class list, and make notes about students' division computation skills.

4 Prepare a *Long Division Learning Contract* activity sheet (pages 67–69) for each student. Students who were able to help solve the real-world problem and successfully compute the quotient on paper will receive the triangle contract. Students who were either able to think through the real-world problem or were able to partially compute the problem on paper will receive the square contract. Students who could not contribute to the class solution of the real-world problem or could not compute the division problem will receive the circle contract.

★ **English Language Support**—Make audio recordings of the activities on the contracts so that English language learners can listen to the directions. Also, make adjustments to any written assignments depending on their language ability levels.

5 For each student, mark the *Long Division Learning Contract Overview* activity sheet (page 66) to indicate which activities must be completed. Attach the appropriate learning contracts to the outlines. Distribute these packets to students. Review the outlines and contracts with students and answer their questions.

6 If students finish their contracts early, they may complete the Anchor Activity.

Long Division Algorithm

Part 1—Reviewing Division with One-Digit Divisors

1 Teach the algorithm for long division. It may be helpful to teach students the *Division Family* mnemonic device. Tell students that they must meet the members of a family in this order: dad (divide), mom (multiply), sister (subtract), brother (bring down), and Rover (remainders). Write these steps and memory aids on the board.

2 Display a simple division problem. Work it slowly as you place a check mark next to each step as you complete it.

3 For guided practice, display sample problems and have students work them in class. Circulate and assist, as needed. Assign computation problems for independent practice.

Part 2—Division with Two-Digit Divisors

1 Review the algorithm for long division. Then, display a division problem with a two-digit divisor. Work it slowly as you place a check mark next to each step as you complete it.

2 For guided practice, display sample problems and have students work them in class. Circulate and assist, as needed. Assign computation problems for independent practice.

Part 3—Division Word Problems

1 Display a division word problem, but do not tell students that division is required. Ask them to read the problem and decide how to solve it. Discuss the clues that helped them recognize the problem as a division problem.

2 Encourage students to share the different strategies which they might use to solve the problem, such as drawing a picture or using the division algorithm. Display several examples of word problems that support this lesson and solve them as a class.

3 Next, ask students to each find a partner for an activity. Each pair of students will write its own real-world division problem and solve it. Collect the problems. Choose several problems to read aloud for the whole class to solve.

Assessment

Evaluate students' performance during mini-lessons, as well as their contract assignment work, to ensure that lesson objectives have been met. Prepare small-group lessons using manipulatives or other division strategies to reteach struggling students.

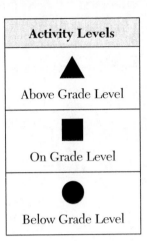

Activity Levels
▲
Above Grade Level
■
On Grade Level
●
Below Grade Level

Anchor Activity

Have students prepare a lesson on division to present to another class or a lower grade. This lesson can be organized as a regular lesson that they as the teacher would teach, or in a book format for them to read aloud.

Name _____

Long Division Learning Contract Overview

Directions: You will participate in the activities checked below. If you do not see a checkmark by an activity, you can use that time to work on the Long Division Learning Contract activities that you have selected.

Part 1—Reviewing Division with One-Digit Divisors

- Review the steps for solving division problems
- Review remainders

  ☐ lesson

  ☐ guided/independent practice of dividing one-digit divisors with remainders

Part 2—Division with Two-Digit Divisors

- Review the steps for solving more complex division problems
- Reinforce division with remainders

  ☐ lesson

  ☐ guided/independent practice of dividing two-digit divisors with remainders

Part 3—Division Word Problems

- Identifying division word problems
- Writing division word problems

  ☐ whole-class lesson

  ☐ guided/independent practice of identifying and writing division word problems

Learning Contract

- Complete any two activities from the learning contract by: _____ .

  ☐ Triangle contract

  ☐ Square contract

  ☐ Circle contract

Name _____

Long Division Learning Contract

Directions: Read the activity choices below. Choose two activities to complete. Fill out the contract with your choices. Then, sign the contract and ask your teacher to sign it, too.

Division Flow Chart

Look at examples of flow charts on the Internet. Then, design your own flow chart to visually show how to solve a division problem step-by-step.

Division Dilemma

Jami, Beth, Kate, and Mia received an inheritance from their great-aunt, Irene. Great-Aunt Irene was quite wealthy, and she loved her grand-nieces dearly. Great-Aunt Irene's estate includes a house, a jewelry collection, a signed original painting, and $110,000 cash. Come up with a way to divide the estate so that each girl gets a fair share. Write a conversation among the four sisters to describe their thinking about this decision. Include the mathematical computations that helped them make their decision.

The Mysterious Link

How is division linked to the concept of fractions? Explore the possible relationships and then find research that proves your ideas. Make an organized list with example problems to describe the link between these two important math concepts.

Schooled in Division

Spend some time researching numerical facts about your school and school district. Find out how many students are enrolled, how large the buildings are, how many staff members are employed, and other little-known data. Then, use the numbers to write five realistic and detailed word problems about your school. Make an answer key on another sheet of paper. Ask a classmate to solve the problems.

I, _____, will complete activities

_____ and _____.

Project due date: _____.

Student signature: _____

Teacher signature: _____

Name _____

Long Division Learning Contract

Directions: Read the activity choices below. Choose two activities to complete. Fill out the contract with your choices. Then, sign the contract and ask your teacher to sign it, too.

Division with the Roll of a Number Cube

Number a sheet of lined paper from 1 to 10. Next to each number, you will create a division number sentence. For each sentence, roll one number cube four times. Use the numbers you roll to create a divisor and a dividend. You may choose to create a three-digit number and a one-digit number, or two two-digit numbers. Make sure the dividend is always larger than the divisor. If it is not, roll one more time and make a three-digit dividend. Solve each problem and check your work.

Division Bingo

Make a division bingo game for classmates to play. Using index cards, create a set of at least 30 problem cards. Use a mixture of easy, average, and challenging division problems. Find the answers to the problems. Then, make four bingo game boards. Write the answers on the boards, but mix them up so that all four boards are different.

Division Decision

The student council is planning a family fun night. The students need to make sure that they have ordered the right amount of food for the 150 people who bought tickets. They are planning to serve pizza, popcorn, and apples. The student council ordered 25 large pizzas. They bought three jars of popcorn kernels and six large bags of apples. Each large pizza has 10 slices. One jar of popcorn kernels makes 25 bags of popcorn. There are 20 apples in a large bag. Use division to find out if the food order needs to be changed. Show your work.

Division Number Stories

Think about your favorite hobby or a subject that interests you. Use realistic numbers related to that subject. Write five division number stories. Add details that make the problems interesting to read and challenging to solve. Make an answer key. Ask a classmate to solve the problems.

I, _____, will complete activities

_____ and _____.

Project due date: _____.

Student signature: _____

Teacher signature: _____

Name _____

Long Division Learning Contract

Directions: Read the activity choices below. Choose two activities to complete. Fill out the contract with your choices. Then, sign the contract and ask your teacher to sign it, too.

Division with the Roll of a Number Cube

Number a sheet of lined paper from 1 to 10. Next to each number, you will make up a division number sentence. For each sentence, roll one number cube three times. Use the numbers you roll to create a one-digit divisor and a two-digit dividend. Solve each problem and check your work.

Division Song

Have you ever had a song stuck in your head? Songs are great memory tools. Write a song about long division to help others remember the steps.

Division Number Stories

Think about your favorite sport or hobby. Use numbers related to that subject. Write three division number stories. Make an answer key. Ask a classmate to solve the problems.

Fact Flash

Using index cards, make a set of division flash cards for the division facts 1 through 12. Use a reliable source to help you. Write the problem on one side of the card and the answer on the other side. Store the set in a plastic bag. Use it to practice your division facts every day.

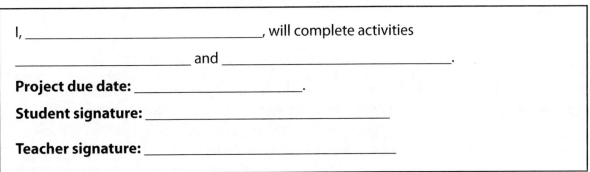

I, _____, will complete activities

_____ and _____.

Project due date: _____.

Student signature: _____

Teacher signature: _____

Equivalent Fractions

Differentiation Strategy

 Tiered Graphic Organizers

Standards

- Students will understand the relative magnitude and relationships among whole numbers, fractions, decimals, and mixed numbers.

- TESOL: Students will use English to obtain, process, construct, and provide subject matter information in spoken and written form.

Materials

- lesson resources (pages 72–75)

- picture books about fractions *(See page 167.)*

- manipulatives, such as fraction strips or circles

Procedures

★ **English Language Support**—Preteach vocabulary related to fractions by reading aloud a picture book about fractions in a small group. The images should provide background information for these students and allow them to participate more fully in the whole-class lesson.

❶ Allow students to choose a partner for an in-class activity. Distribute a set of manipulatives, such as fraction strips or fraction circles, to each pair. Allow time for students to explore the manipulatives.

❷ Write the word *equivalent* on the board. Pronounce it. Ask students to identify a familiar word that sounds like the vocabulary term. The correct response is *equal*. Explain that equivalent fractions are fractions that are equal to each other.

❸ Ask students to name equivalent fractions. Write their responses on the board. This will help you gauge students' understanding of the concept.

❹ Write simple equivalent fractions on the board one at a time. Have each pair use the manipulatives to show that the two fractions are equivalent. Circulate around the room and check students' responses.

❺ Most manipulatives show the *parts of a whole* fraction model. Use data about the students in the class to make up engaging *parts of a set* problems. For example, say that $\frac{8}{24}$ *or* $\frac{1}{3}$ *of the students in the class are wearing sneakers or* $\frac{24}{24}$ *or* $\frac{1}{1}$ *(all) students in the class are fifth graders.* Have students act out the examples by moving into the correct groups.

Equivalent Fractions

6 Distribute copies of the *Finding Equivalent Fractions* activity sheet (page 72) to students. Show students how to find equivalent fractions for any fraction by multiplying or dividing the numerator and denominator by the same number. Tell students that there is an important rule to remember when working with fractions: *Whatever you do to the numerator, you must do to the denominator (and vice versa).* Have students complete the activity sheet. Circulate and assist as needed.

7 Divide the class into homogeneous groups of three or four students for more practice with equivalent fractions. Distribute copies of the *Equivalent Fractions* activity sheets (pages 73–75) to students based on their readiness levels.

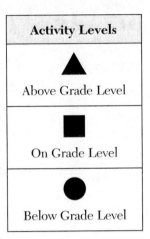

Activity Levels
▲
Above Grade Level
■
On Grade Level
●
Below Grade Level

8 Allow time for groups to complete the tiered graphic organizers. Have groups compare their responses with other groups at the same level.

9 If students finish early, they may complete the Anchor Activity.

Anchor Activity

Have students write three to five word problems using equivalent fractions in real-world situations. Make sure they also make answer keys.

Assessment

Evaluate students' graphic organizers to be sure that they are working at the appropriate levels and understand the concepts that have been taught.

Name _____

Finding Equivalent Fractions

Directions: To find equivalent fractions, multiply or divide the numerator and denominator of the original fraction by a fraction equal to one whole. This new fraction is equivalent to the original fraction.

Example: $\dfrac{1}{2} \times \dfrac{2}{2} = \dfrac{2}{4}$

Original Fraction	x or ÷	=
$\dfrac{1}{3}$	x $\dfrac{2}{2}$	$\dfrac{2}{6}$
$\dfrac{2}{7}$	x $\dfrac{3}{3}$	$\dfrac{6}{21}$
$\dfrac{3}{8}$		
$\dfrac{1}{4}$		
$\dfrac{4}{5}$		
$\dfrac{36}{108}$	÷ $\dfrac{3}{3}$	$\dfrac{12}{36}$
	÷ $\dfrac{2}{2}$	$\dfrac{3}{6}$
	÷ $\dfrac{10}{10}$	$\dfrac{10}{100}$
	÷ $\dfrac{25}{25}$	$\dfrac{25}{75}$

Name _____

Equivalent Fractions

Directions: Start with the fractions given below. For each fraction, make three equivalent fractions. Complete the chart below. A sample has been provided for you.

Original Fraction	x or ÷	Equivalent Fraction	x or ÷	Equivalent Fraction	x or ÷	Equivalent Fraction
$\frac{2}{10}$	$\times \frac{10}{10}$	$\frac{20}{100}$	$\times \frac{2}{2}$	$\frac{40}{200}$	$\div \frac{4}{4}$	$\frac{10}{50}$
		$\frac{24}{48}$				
$\frac{4}{16}$						
		$\frac{25}{50}$				
$\frac{3}{5}$						

Name _____

Equivalent Fractions

Directions: Start with any fractions of your choice. For each fraction, multiply or divide to make two equivalent fractions. Complete the chart below. A sample has been provided for you.

Original Fraction	x or ÷	Equivalent Fraction	x or ÷	Equivalent Fraction
$\frac{1}{3}$	x $\frac{2}{2}$	$\frac{2}{6}$	x $\frac{3}{3}$	$\frac{6}{18}$

Name _____

Equivalent Fractions

Directions: Start with the original fractions below. Multiply or divide to make an equivalent fraction. Complete the chart below. Two samples have been provided for you.

Original Fraction	x or ÷	Equivalent Fraction
$\dfrac{1}{2}$	x $\dfrac{2}{2}$	= $\dfrac{2}{4}$
$\dfrac{12}{12}$	÷ $\dfrac{4}{4}$	= $\dfrac{3}{3}$
$\dfrac{6}{8}$		
$\dfrac{2}{3}$		
$\dfrac{4}{16}$		
$\dfrac{1}{3}$		
$\dfrac{25}{35}$		
$\dfrac{8}{9}$		

Exploring Volume

Differentiation Strategy

Tiered Assignments

Standards

- Students will understand the basic measures of perimeter, area, volume, capacity, mass, angle, and circumference.

- TESOL: Students will use English to obtain, process, construct, and provide subject matter information in spoken and written form.

Materials

- lesson resources (pages 78–81)

- centimeter cubes

- 5–10 small boxes

- rulers

- variety of building materials, such as newspaper, cardboard, card stock, origami paper, glue, tape, staplers, and paper clips

Procedures

1 Begin the lesson with a review of the concepts of perimeter and area. Show real-life examples and review the two formulas. Build on that understanding as you move on to the concept of volume.

2 Place students in small heterogeneous groups. Give each group a pile of centimeter cubes and a small box. Make sure the groups have boxes in different sizes and shapes to yield a variety of different measurements.

3 Ask students to use the centimeter cubes to find the perimeter of the bottom of the box. The easiest way to do this is to place the cubes inside the box and count how many can be arranged along the sides. Have students record the perimeter.

4 Have students find the area and record it. Some groups may cover the bottom of the box with cubes to find the area and others may use the formula for area. Either method is fine.

5 Write the word *volume* on the board. Invite students to share what they know about this term. Reinforce the idea that volume is the amount of space a three-dimensional object occupies. Ask students how they would find the volume of the box in front of them by using the centimeter cubes. Have students share their strategies. Some groups may fill the box with cubes and count each cube. Other groups may realize that if they stack the cubes in the corner of the box, they can figure out how many levels it will take to fill it and will multiply the amount in one level by the number of total levels.

6 Remind students that the formula for the area of a rectangle (a two-dimensional shape) is *length × width*. Then, write the formula for the *volume* of a rectangular prism (a three-dimensional shape), which is *length × width × height*, on the board. Help students see the connection between the two formulas.

7 Now ask groups to switch boxes. Have students use manipulatives and formulas to find the perimeter, area, and volume of a second box. Repeat this activity as many times as you wish.

Exploring Volume

8 For independent practice, distribute copies of the *Exploring Volume* activity sheet (pages 78–80) to students based on their readiness levels.

★ **English Language Support**—Pair these students with partners at their readiness levels. Ahead of time, provide tips for the partners about working with English language learners. Advise them to speak slowly and clearly, and to point to words as they read aloud. Ask them to allow extra time for their partners to respond to questions. Remind them that these students are bright and capable but face challenges learning a new language.

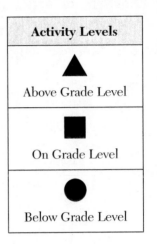

Activity Levels	
▲	Above Grade Level
■	On Grade Level
●	Below Grade Level

9 As an extension, distribute copies of the *Volume Challenge* activity sheet (page 81) to students. For this hands-on challenge, students will build models of cubic units. Provide rulers and building materials such as newspaper, cardboard, card stock, origami paper, glue, tape, staplers, and paper clips. Let students work with partners to figure out how to construct the models.

Anchor Activity ⚓

Have students find the volume of 10 rectangular prisms in the classroom or around the school.

10 If students finish early, they may complete the Anchor Activity.

Assessment

Evaluate students' activity sheets to be sure that they are working at the appropriate levels and understand the concepts that have been taught.

Name _____

Exploring Volume

Directions: Complete the problems below. You will need a small box and centimeter cubes. Answer problems 3 and 4 on a separate sheet of paper.

1. In the space below, outline the bottom of the box. Use centimeter cubes to find the perimeter, area, and volume of the box. Show your work.

Perimeter = _____ Area = _____ Volume = _____

2. Complete the table below. Use what you know about the formulas for area and volume to find the missing data.

Length	Width	Height	Area	Volume
3 ft.	4 ft.	2 ft.		
10 in.	12 in.	5 in.		
9 yd.	_____ yd.	2 yd.	63 yd.²	_____ yd.³
_____ in.	3 in.	8 in.	9 in.²	72 in.³

3. Explain how to find the length, width, and height of a box given the following information:

    The area of the base of the box is 25 square inches. The perimeter of the base is 20 inches.

    The volume of the box is 175 cubic inches.

4. Write a word problem using what you have learned about volume. Write the answer upside down on the back of this sheet.

Name _____

Exploring Volume

Directions: Complete the problems below. You will need a small box and centimeter cubes.

1. In the space below, outline the bottom of the box. Use centimeter cubes to find the length, width, and height of the box.

Length = _____   Width = _____   Height = _____

2. To find the perimeter, use the formula _____.

   The perimeter of the box = _____.

   To find the area, use the formula _____.

   The area of the box = _____.

3. To find the volume, use the formula _____.

   The volume of the box = _____.

4. Complete the table below. Use what you know about the formulas for area and volume to find the missing data.

Length	Width	Height	Area	Volume
5 ft.	7 ft.	2 ft.	35 ft.^{2}	
6 yd.	4 yd.	5 yd.		
9 in.	2 in.	2 in.		
3 ft.	_____ ft.	6 ft.	6 ft.^{2}	36 ft.^{3}

Name _____

Exploring Volume

Directions: Complete the problems below. You will need a small box and centimeter cubes.

1. In the space below, outline the bottom of the box. Use centimeter cubes to find the length, width, and height of the box.

Length = _____ Width = _____ Height = _____

2. To find the perimeter, use the formula *side + side + side + side*.

   The perimeter of the box = _____cm.

3. To find the area, use the formula *length × width*.

   The area of the box = _____cm².

4. To find the volume, use the formula *length × width × height*.

   The volume of the box = _____cm³.

5. Complete the table below. Use what you know about the formulas for area and volume to find the missing data.

Length	Width	Height	Area	Volume
2 ft.	3 ft.	2 ft.	_____ ft.²	12 ft.³
4 in.	2 in.	3 in.	8 in.²	_____ in.³
5 in.	5 in.	2 in.	_____ in.²	_____ in.³
6 ft.	2 ft.	2 ft.	_____ ft.²	_____ ft.³

Name _____

Volume Challenge

Directions: Use the materials provided to make models of one cubic centimeter, one cubic foot, one cubic inch, and one cubic meter. Complete the project sheet below.

1. Before constructing the models, predict their sizes in relation to one other. List the models from the smallest to the largest.

   _____   _____   _____   _____

2. How do you plan to complete this challenge? List the steps that you will take.

   _____

   _____

   _____

   _____

   _____

3. What was the most challenging part of this project? Explain your answer.

   _____

   _____

   _____

4. Write three word problems using the models that you created.

   _____

   _____

   _____

   _____

   _____

   _____

   _____

   _____

Geometry Wrap-Up

Differentiation Strategy

 Menu of Options

Standards

• Students will understand and apply basic and advanced properties of the concepts of geometry.

• TESOL: Students will use appropriate learning strategies to construct and apply academic knowledge.

Materials

• lesson resources (pages 84–87)

• chart paper and markers

• rulers

• protractors

• timer

• books and websites about the art of M. C. Escher, origami, and symmetry (See page 167.)

• drawing software

• art supplies

• grid paper

• digital camera

• tangram templates

• scissors

Procedures

Note: This lesson is designed as a conclusion to a geometry unit. Projects from the menu of options are a fitting unit assessment. The rubric provided with this lesson will help you assess the projects accurately and quickly.

Preparation Note: Draw four large shapes or designs on chart paper. Choose shapes and designs that include as many concepts as possible from the unit. As you draw, think about different shapes, angles, types of lines, symmetry, and the concept of congruent/similar. Leave space on and around the drawings for students to write. Post the papers in different locations around the classroom. Place rulers and protractors near each chart paper design.

★ **English Language Support**—Prior to the lesson, make a word wall of geometry terms on chart paper. Include simple definitions and labeled illustrations. Encourage English language learners to use this tool during the in-class review and while working on their projects.

❶ Place students in five heterogeneous groups for a geometry review game. Give each group a different color marker. Assign each group an answering order so that each student will participate at regular intervals. Have English language learners and below-grade-level students go first. This will give them a chance to name the more obvious facts about the designs while challenging students who go after them to think of less obvious facts.

❷ Tell students that you want to see what they have learned about geometry. Point out the designs on chart paper around the room. Explain that students will take turns writing facts, vocabulary words, and measurements on the designs. Encourage students to be clever and accurate in their answers. Since each team has a different color marker, you will be able to see which team recalled the most facts. This team will win the game.

Geometry Wrap-Up

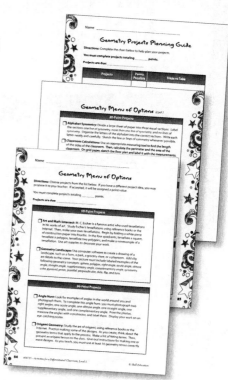

3 Set a timer for 10 or 15 minutes. Play the review game for the whole time. Encourage students to continue writing facts until time is up. Offer whole-class hints as needed. After the game, count the responses from each team and celebrate the winners.

4 Students will show what they know about geometry by completing projects chosen from the *Geometry Menu of Options* activity sheets (pages 84–85). Decide ahead of time the number of points students need to complete from the menu and determine a due date. Students may propose additional projects for extra credit.

5 Have students use the *Geometry Projects Planning Guide* activity sheet (page 86) to organize their choices. Assist students in making appropriate selections. Provide students with any needed materials to help them complete the activities.

6 If students finish early, they may complete the Anchor Activity.

Assessment

Use the *Geometry Projects Rubric* (page 87) to assess students' projects. You may need to make more than one copy per student, depending on the point requirements for the assignment.

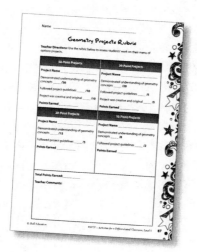

Anchor Activity

Have students design a new project to add to the menu of options. Ask them to plan the project details in writing. Then, have them complete the project. Use their work as a sample to show future students.

Name _____

Geometry Menu of Options

Directions: Choose projects from the list below. If you have a different project idea, you may propose it to your teacher. If accepted, it will be assigned a point value.

You must complete projects totaling _____ points.

Projects are due: _____

50-Point Projects

☐ **Art and Math Intersect:** M. C. Escher is a famous artist who used tessellations in his works of art. Study Escher's tessellations using reference books or the Internet. Then, make your own tessellations. Begin by folding a white piece of construction paper into fourths. In the four quadrants, tessellate a square, tessellate a polygon, tessellate two polygons, and make a nonexample of a tessellation. Use art supplies to decorate your work.

☐ **Geometry Landscape:** Use computer software to create a drawing of a landscape, such as a farm, a park, a grocery store, or a playroom. Add clip art details to the scene. Your picture must include labeled examples of the following geometry concepts: *sphere, polygon, right angle, acute angle, obtuse angle, straight angle, supplementary angle, complementary angle, symmetry, cube, pyramid, prism, parallel, perpendicular, slide, flip, and turn.*

30-Point Projects

☐ **Angle Hunt:** Look for examples of angles in the world around you and photograph them. To complete this angle hunt, you must photograph two right angles, one acute angle, one obtuse angle, one straight angle, one supplementary angle, and one complementary angle. Print the photos, measure the angles with a protractor, and label them. Display your work on an eye-catching poster.

☐ **Origami Geometry:** Study the art of origami, using reference books or the Internet. Practice making some of the designs. As you create, think about the geometry terms that apply to the process. Make a list of fitting terms. Then, present an origami lesson to the class. Give oral instructions for making one or more designs. As you teach, you must use at least 10 geometry terms correctly.

Geometry Menu of Options *(cont.)*

20-Point Projects

☐ **Alphabet Symmetry:** Divide a large sheet of paper into three equal sections. Label the sections *one line of symmetry, more than one line of symmetry,* and *no lines of symmetry.* Organize the letters of the alphabet into the correct sections. Write each letter neatly and carefully. Sketch the line or lines of symmetry whenever possible.

☐ **Classroom Calculations:** Use an appropriate measuring tool to find the length of the sides of the classroom. Then, calculate the perimeter and the area of the classroom. On grid paper, sketch the floor plan and label it with the measurements. Next, choose another room and repeat the procedure.

☐ **Artistic Angles:** Use a ruler and markers to draw a geometric design on a large piece of paper. Then, measure and label at least 20 angles in the picture. Each label must include the measurement and all names that apply to the angle.

10-Point Projects

☐ **Tangram Puzzles:** You will need a piece of paper, scissors, and a ruler. Carefully cut out seven tangrams. Rearrange all seven to form a square and then a triangle. Next, use five pieces to form a triangle. Use three pieces to form a trapezoid. Then, make two designs of your own. For each design, trace around the shapes to show exactly how you put the pieces together.

☐ **Natural Symmetry:** Read about symmetry, using reference books or the Internet. Then, identify five symmetrical forms in nature. Sketch pictures of the examples and draw their lines of symmetry.

☐ **Career Choices:** Make a list of at least 10 jobs that require workers to use geometry on a daily basis. Explain in one or two sentences how geometry applies to each job.

Student-Proposed Projects

☐ _____

_____

_____

☐ _____

_____

_____

Geometry Projects Planning Guide

Directions: Complete the chart below to help plan your projects.

You must complete projects totaling _____ points.

Projects are due: _____

Projects	Points Possible	Steps to Take
Total Points:		

#50737—*Activities for a Differentiated Classroom, Level 5*

Name _____

Geometry Projects Rubric

Teacher Directions: Use the rubric below to assess students' work on their menu of options projects.

50-Point Projects	30-Point Projects
Project Name _____	**Project Name** _____
Demonstrated understanding of geometry concepts _____ **/30**	Demonstrated understanding of geometry concepts _____ **/20**
Followed project guidelines _____ **/10**	Followed project guidelines _____ **/5**
Project was creative and original _____ **/10**	Project was creative and original _____ **/5**
Points Earned _____	**Points Earned** _____
20-Point Projects	**10-Point Projects**
Project Name _____	**Project Name** _____
Demonstrated understanding of geometry concepts _____ **/15**	Demonstrated understanding of geometry concepts _____ **/8**
Followed project guidelines _____ **/5**	Followed project guidelines _____ **/2**
Points Earned _____	**Points Earned** _____

Total Points Earned: _____

Teacher Comments:

Introducing Algebra

Differentiation Strategy

 Bloom's Taxonomy

Standard

• Students will know that a variable is a letter or symbol that stands for one or more numbers.

• TESOL: Students will use English to obtain, process, construct, and provide subject matter information in spoken and written form.

Materials

• lesson resources (pages 90–93)

• toothpicks

• audio software

Procedures

❶ Tell students that they will be learning algebra today. This is exciting for many students, so reflect excitement back to them as you begin the lesson. Tell students that algebra is not as scary as it looks. The letters are simply unknown numbers. In other words, a letter in a math problem is the same as a blank line or empty box; it simply means that you do not know what goes in that place yet. Write the following equations on the board. Ask students to solve for the unknowns. Invite students to explain their thinking as they volunteer answers. *(n = 3; h = 8; a = 2)*

$$n + 5 = 8 \quad h + 4 = 12 \quad 9 + a = 11$$

❷ Tell students that the letters are called *variables*. Explain that the letters are chosen randomly, or they might stand for something in the problem. For example, if you are solving for the amount of money earned, you might use *m* for *money*.

❸ Explain that tables are a good way to organize mathematical data in order to solve problems in algebra. They help you to see relationships between the numbers. From a relationship, you make a mathematical rule to use in solving problems.

❹ Display the *Algebraic Patterns* activity sheet (page 90), and distribute copies to students. Examine the first table together as a class. Look for the pattern in each column. What is being done to the number in the *x* column to to make the number in the *y* column? *(The rule is x + 4 = y)*

x	Rule	y
1		5
2		6
3		7
5		
10		

Introducing Algebra

⑤ Have students complete the second table independently. *(The rule is $x \times 4 = y$)*

x	Rule	y
1		4
2		8
3		12
5		
10		

⑥ Have students complete the third table independently. *(The rule is $x \div 2 = y$)*

x	Rule	y
4		2
8		4
12		6
16		
20		

Activity Levels
▲
Above Grade Level
■
On Grade Level
●
Below Grade Level

⑦ Distribute copies of the *Questions About Algebra* activity sheets (pages 91–93) to students based on their readiness levels. Above-grade-level students should work independently. On-grade-level students should choose a partner with the same sheet. Below-grade-level students should work with you in a small group. Provide students with enough toothpicks to help them complete the activity.

★ **English Language Support**—Create a podcast in which you read aloud the directions and questions. Allow English language learners to listen to the podcast as they work.

⑧ If students finish early, they may complete the Anchor Activity.

Assessment

Evaluate students' activity sheets to be sure that they are working at the appropriate levels and understand the concepts that have been taught.

Anchor Activity

Have students create five more *What Is the Rule?* tables. Encourage them to make these tables as challenging as possible. Ask them to submit an answer key with their work.

Name _____

Algebraic Patterns

Directions: Study the tables below. What patterns do you see? How do the numbers in the *x* column relate to the numbers in the *y* column? Use the patterns to complete the tables and find the rules.

x	Rule	*y*
1		5
2		6
3		7
5		
10		

1. What is the rule?

_____

x	Rule	*y*
1		4
2		8
3		12
5		
10		

2. What is the rule?

_____

x	Rule	*y*
4		2
8		4
12		6
16		
20		

3. What is the rule?

_____

Name _____

Questions About Algebra

Directions: Use seven toothpicks to create the design below. Then, answer the questions that follow.

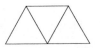

1. **Understanding:** Use information from the toothpick design to complete the table.

Number of Triangles	Number of Toothpicks
1	
2	
3	7
4	
5	
6	
7	

2. **Understanding:** Predict how many toothpicks will be needed to create a chain of

    20 triangles: _____, 50 triangles: _____, 100 triangles: _____

3. **Applying:** Write a rule in words and variables that explains the pattern. _____

    _____

4. **Applying:** Look at the three steps in the pattern. Then, draw the next step in the pattern.

    Step 1:

    Step 2:

    Step 3:

    Step 4:

5. **Creating:** Use toothpicks to create a pattern design of your own. Sketch the design on the back of this paper. What rule does the pattern follow? Draw a table to record the relationship.

6. **Creating:** On the back of this page, write five algebra problems about your design.

Name _____

Questions About Algebra

Directions: Use seven toothpicks to create the design below. Then, answer the questions that follow.

Number of Triangles	Number of Toothpicks
3	7
4	
5	
6	
7	
8	
9	

1. **Understanding:** Look at the table. Continue to add toothpicks to the triangle design to follow the pattern. Complete the table as you work.

2. **Understanding:** Describe the pattern in the table. _____

   _____

3. **Understanding:** Predict how many toothpicks will be needed to create a chain of

   15 triangles: _____,   20 triangles: _____

4. **Applying:** Write a rule in words and variables that explains the pattern. _____

   _____

5. **Applying:** Look at the three steps in the pattern. On the back of this page, draw the next step in the pattern.

   Step 1: ▢▢   Step 2: ▢▢▢   Step 3: ▢▢▢▢▢▢

Step	Number of Squares
1	2
2	4
3	6
4	
5	
6	

6. **Applying:** Complete the table to find the pattern between the step number and the number of squares.

7. **Applying:** How many squares will there be on Step 10? _____ Step 20? _____

8. **Applying:** Write a rule in words and variables that explains the pattern. _____

Name _____

Questions About Algebra

Directions: Use seven toothpicks to create the design below. Then, answer the questions that follow.

Number of Triangles	Rule	Number of Toothpicks
3		7
4		
5		
6		
7		
8		
9		

1. **Understanding:** Look at the table. Continue to add toothpicks to the triangle design to follow the pattern. Complete the table as you work.

2. **Understanding:** Describe the pattern in the table. _____

    _____

3. **Understanding:** Predict how many toothpicks will be needed to create a chain of

    10 triangles: _____,   11 triangles: _____

4. **Applying:** What do you do to the numbers in the first column to find the number in the second column? Write the rule. _____

5. **Applying:** Look at the three steps in the pattern below. Complete the table to chart the pattern between the step number and the number of squares.

    Step 1: ☐☐   Step 2: ☐☐☐☐   Step 3: ☐☐☐☐☐☐

Step Number	Rule	Number of Squares
1		2
2		4
3		6
4		
5		

6. **Applying:** What do you do to the numbers in the first column to make the number in the second column? Write the rule. _____

    _____

The Scientific Method

Differentiation Strategy

 Leveled Learning Contracts

Standards

- Students will plan and conduct simple investigations.
- TESOL: Students will use appropriate learning strategies to construct and apply academic knowledge.

Materials

- lesson resources (page 96–99)
- scissors
- cups
- baking soda
- water
- lemonade
- spoons, teaspoons
- apple juice
- orange juice
- lemon-lime soda
- glue sticks
- science notebooks
- envelopes

Procedures

❶ Find out what students know about the Scientific Method by doing a quick informal evaluation. This can be done by asking students the following questions: *What is the Scientific Method? List the steps of the Scientific Method. What is a hypothesis? In the field of science, what is a fair test?*

❷ Evaluate students' answers and assign them to the appropriate *Scientific Method Learning Contract* activity sheet (pages 97–99). Students who answer all questions correctly receive the triangle contract. Students who miss one or two questions receive the square contract. Students who miss more than two questions receive the circle contract.

❸ Distribute the contracts to students. Review the contracts with the class.

★ **English Language Support**—Meet with these students in a small group to clarify their contract instructions.

❹ If students finish their learning contracts early, they may complete the Anchor Activity.

Part 1

Preparation Note: Make enough copies of *The Scientific Method* activity sheet (page 96) for each student participating in this lesson. Cut the six steps apart and place them in an envelope. Have glue sticks and students' science notebooks on hand.

❶ Students with the square and circle contracts will join you for this first lesson. Students with triangle contracts will work independently on their learning contracts.

❷ Distribute the envelopes with *The Scientific Method* strips to students. Have students read each strip and try to put the steps in the correct order. When everyone has attempted to order the strips, display the correct order. Have students glue the strips into their science notebooks in the correct order.

❸ Explain that the Scientific Method is the way in which scientists all over the world approach their work. It is a way of thinking about science. Review the steps of the Scientific Method. Have students work in pairs to come up with mnemonic devices to help them remember the steps in order.

The Scientific Method

Part 2

① Only students with the circle contracts will join you for this lesson. Students with triangle and square contracts will work independently.

② Pass out a small cup of lemon-lime soda to each student. Have students use their five senses to make observations about the liquid.

③ Then, work with students to write a question about the bubbles in the soda. At this point, students will begin using the Scientific Method. Have students copy the question into their science notebooks under the title *Fizzy Drinks*.

④ This simple experiment uses baking soda, water, and lemonade to make fizzy drinks. Display the ingredients. Tell students about the properties of baking soda and lemonade.

⑤ Ask students to make notes about their background research in their science notebooks. Then, have the whole group work together to form a hypothesis. Write students' ideas on the board. Circle the final choice. Instruct students to record the hypothesis in their science notebooks.

⑥ Place students in pairs. Distribute two cups, two spoons, $\frac{1}{2}$ teaspoon of baking soda, 1 cup of lemonade, and 1 cup of water to each student. Instruct students to fill one cup half full of water and stir in $\frac{1}{2}$ teaspoon of baking soda. Have them fill the second cup half full of lemonade. Use a clean spoon to put $\frac{1}{2}$ teaspoon of baking soda in the lemonade. Have students describe the results in their science notebooks.

⑦ Work together as a whole group to draw a conclusion about the experiment. Have students copy this conclusion into their science notebooks. Then, help students plan a way to communicate their experiment results with the class.

Assessment

Evaluate students' activity sheets to be sure that they are working at the appropriate levels and understand the concepts that have been taught.

Activity Levels
▲
Above Grade Level
■
On Grade Level
●
Below Grade Level

Anchor Activity

Have students study the work of professional scientists in a field that interests them, such as space, medicine, or nature. Provide access to scientific journals. Challenge students to identify the steps of the Scientific Method in the work of these published scientists.

Name _____

The Scientific Method

Teacher Directions: Use copies of this sheet for Lesson 1. Cut apart the steps of the Scientific Method and place them in an envelope for each student.

Ask a Question
Let your curiosity inspire you. Observe the world around you and allow yourself to wonder how and why.

Do Background Research
Read about the topic. Spend time observing the subject.

Form a Hypothesis
Answer your question with an educated guess. Write your prediction as a statement.

Conduct an Experiment
Design a fair test that could be repeated by anyone.

Draw Conclusions
Analyze your data and decide if your hypothesis was true or false.

Communicate Results
Call a friend, present it to the class, create a blog, or write a paper. Real scientists share their work with other scientists. They tell them specific details so that they can try the experiment, too.

 #50737—*Activities for a Differentiated Classroom, Level 5*

Name _____

Scientific Method Learning Contract

Directions: Think about observations you have made about the world around you. Then, think about the questions that came from those observations. Now, design and carry out an experiment inspired by your own curiosity.

The Scientific Method

Step 1: _____
_____

Step 2: _____
_____
_____

Step 3: _____
_____

Step 4: _____
_____
_____
_____
_____

Step 5: _____
_____
_____

Step 6: _____
_____

How can your teacher help you with this project? _____
_____
_____

How can an adult at home help you with this project? _____
_____

Project Due Date: _____

Student Signature: _____

Parent/Guardian Signature: _____

Teacher Signature: _____

Name _____

Scientific Method Learning Contract

Directions: Follow the steps in the Scientific Method to conduct an experiment on your own. Make notes about each step as you work.

Observation: *Some drinks are fizzy and have bubbles in them. Other drinks do not.*

The Scientific Method

Step 1: _____

_____

_____

_____

Step 2: _____

_____

_____

_____

_____

Step 3: _____

_____

Step 4: Conduct an Experiment

Each scientist needs: two cups, two spoons, 1 teaspoon of baking soda, 1 cup of lemonade, and 1 cup of water

Experimental design—Fill one cup half full of water. Stir $\frac{1}{2}$ teaspoon of baking soda into the water. Fill the second cup half full of lemonade. Use a clean spoon to put $\frac{1}{2}$ teaspoon of baking soda in the lemonade.

Step 5: _____

_____

_____

_____

Step 6: _____

_____

Project Due Date: _____

Student Signature: _____

Teacher Signature: _____

Challenge: If time allows, repeat this experiment with apple juice and orange juice. Compare these results to the results of the lemonade test.

Name _____

Scientific Method Learning Contract

Directions: Follow the directions in Step 4 to conduct an experiment. Make notes about the Scientific Method as you work.

Observation: *Some drinks are fizzy and have bubbles in them. Other drinks do not.*

The Scientific Method

Step 1: Ask a Question _____

_____

_____

Step 2: Do Background Research _____

_____

_____

_____

_____

Step 3: Form a Hypothesis _____

_____

Step 4: Conduct an Experiment

Each scientist needs: two cups, two spoons, 1 teaspoon of baking soda, 1 cup of apple juice, and 1 cup of orange juice

Experimental design: Fill one cup half full of apple juice. Stir $\frac{1}{2}$ teaspoon of baking soda into the apple juice. Fill the second cup half full of orange juice. Use a clean spoon to put $\frac{1}{2}$ a teaspoon of baking powder in the orange juice.

Step 5: Draw Conclusions _____

_____

_____

_____

Step 6: Communicate Results _____

_____

Project Due Date: _____

Student Signature: _____

Teacher Signature: _____

Rock Investigation

Differentiation Strategy

 Tiered Assignments

Standards

- Students will know that rock is composed of different combinations of minerals.

- TESOL: Students will use appropriate learning strategies to construct and apply academic knowledge.

Materials

- lesson resources (pages 102–105)
- crayon shavings
- heavy aluminum foil
- chart paper and markers
- video clips of rock cycle
- books to use as weights
- candle and matches
- sandpaper
- different types of rocks
- magnifying lens
- penny
- butter knife
- steel nail
- glass
- magnet

Procedures

Preparation Note: Shave crayons of different colors onto a sheet of heavy aluminum foil. Fold the aluminum foil to create a lip around its edges to contain the crayon shavings.

❶ Ask students to name and describe cycles in nature (water cycle, food chain, phases of the moon, etc.). Ask students if they have ever heard of the rock cycle. Then, invite students to share any facts that they know about rocks and how rocks are formed. Record students' ideas on the board or on chart paper.

❷ Explain that the rock cycle is another cycle in nature. The rock cycle explains how different types of rocks are formed. There are five stages or steps in the rock cycle. Distribute copies of *The Rock Cycle* activity sheet (page 102). Point out the five types of rocks—*sediments, sedimentary rock, metamorphic rock, magma,* and *igneous rock*. Point out the processes that form the types of rocks—*compaction and cementation; heat and pressure; melting; cooling; weathering and erosion*.

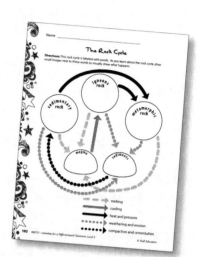

★ **English Language Support**—Show video clips of the stages of the rock cycle. This will catch students' attention and provide background knowledge for these students to connect with the new vocabulary terms.

❸ Divide the class into small, heterogeneous groups. Give each group an aluminum foil tray with crayon shavings.

❹ Ask students to guess which stage of the rock cycle the crayon shavings represent (sediment). Make sure all students understand the connection between sediment and the crayon shavings.

5 Have students cover the crayon shavings with another sheet of foil. Then, have them use medium-weight books to apply pressure to the crayon shaving "sediment." Ask students to explain what they see. The crayon sediment has cemented into a solid form, a sedimentary rock. Ask students to make observations about sedimentary rocks.

6 Have students use heavy-weight books to apply heavy pressure to the "sedimentary rock" shavings overnight. If possible, apply heat by placing the experiment near a heating vent or a heat light. Have students check their "rocks" the following day to see if more changes can be observed. The stronger rocks that are formed by heat and heavy pressure are metamorphic rocks.

7 Place the crayon "rocks" back onto the foil. Demonstrate what happens to the rocks when heat is applied by placing a foil tray over a candle. This *melting* phase of the rock cycle causes rocks to become magma. Melt each group's "rock" so that students can make observations about this stage.

8 As the magma cools, it crystallizes and becomes igneous rock. Ask students to report their observations on this phase.

9 Finally, have students rub their igneous rocks against sandpaper. This demonstrates weathering and erosion. Have the students report their observations as the rocks turn back into sediment. This completes the rock cycle.

10 Students will investigate a rock. You may wish to number the rock samples you provide for ease of reference. Distribute copies of the *Rock Investigation* activity sheets (pages 103–105) to students based on their readiness levels. Circulate around the room and assist students as needed. Provide students with any needed materials to help them complete the activities.

11 If students finish early, they may complete the Anchor Activity.

Assessment

Observe students as they experiment with the rocks. Evaluate students' work to be sure that they are working at the appropriate levels and understand the concepts that have been taught.

Activity Levels
▲
Above Grade Level
■
On Grade Level
●
Below Grade Level

Anchor Activity

Have students find photos of the stages of the rock cycle. Have them compile these into a slide show presentation or a poster to visually show the stages of the rock cycle.

Name _____

The Rock Cycle

Directions: This rock cycle is labeled with words. As you learn about the rock cycle, draw small images next to these words to visually show what happens.

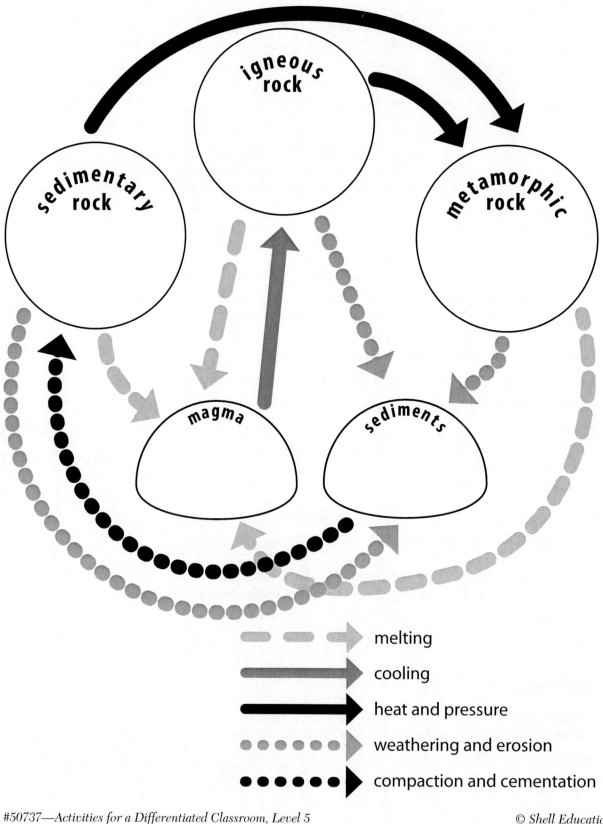

melting

cooling

heat and pressure

weathering and erosion

compaction and cementation

Name _____

Rock Investigation

Part 1
Directions: Select a rock. Investigate the rock by completing all the tests below.

Test 1: Describe It

Look at your rock carefully. Note the color, patterns, shape, crystals, and other features.

_____

_____

Test 2: Magnify It

Use a magnifying lens to look at your rock. On the back of this paper, sketch a detailed view of your rock under magnification.

Test 3: Identify It

What type of rock is it? Explain your answer. _____

_____

Test 4: Scratch It

Find out how hard your rock is by trying these tests. Assign the rock a hardness number based on the tests below. Scale Number: _____

Scale	1	2	3	4	5	6	7	8–10
Scratch Test	Leaves a mark when rubbed on the skin	Can be scratched by a fingernail	Can be scratched by a penny	Can be scratched easily by a butter knife	Can be scratched by a butter knife after much effort	Can be scratched with a steel nail but not glass	Can scratch glass	Too hard to be tested on this scale

Test 5: Attract It

Use a magnet to test if your rock contains magnetic material. Describe what happened.

_____

Part 2
Directions: Write a creative story about your rock's history. Personify your rock with a name and an interesting life story. Include scientific facts about the rock cycle and creative details. If time allows, turn your story into a picture book or an animated movie.

Name _____

Rock Investigation

Part 1
Directions: Select a rock. Investigate the rock by completing all the tests below.

Test 1: Describe It

Look at your rock carefully. Describe the color, patterns, shape, crystals, and other features.

_____

_____

Test 2: Magnify It

Use a magnifying lens to look at your rock. On the back of this paper, sketch a detailed view of your rock under magnification.

Test 3: Identify It

Is it a sedimentary, metamorphic, or igneous rock? Explain your answer. _____

_____

Test 4: Scratch It

Find out how hard your rock is by trying these tests. Assign the rock a hardness number based on the tests below. Scale Number: _____

Scale	1	2	3	4	5	6	7	8–10
Scratch Test	Leaves a mark when rubbed on the skin	Can be scratched by a fingernail	Can be scratched by a penny	Can be scratched easily by a butter knife	Can be scratched by a butter knife after much effort	Can be scratched with a steel nail but not glass	Can scratch glass	Too hard to be tested on this scale

Test 5: Attract It

Use a magnet to test if your rock contains magnetic material. Describe what happened.

_____

Part 2
Directions: Write and illustrate a comic strip about the life of your rock. Give the rock a name and an interesting story. Include facts about the rock cycle and creative details.

Name _____

Rock Investigation

Part 1
Directions: Select a rock. Investigate the rock by completing all the tests below.

Test 1: Describe It

What color is the rock? _____

What patterns do you see on the rock? _____

Describe the shape of the rock: _____

What other things do you notice about the way the rock looks? _____

Test 2: Magnify It

Use a magnifying lens to look at your rock. On the back of this paper, sketch a detailed view of your rock under magnification.

Test 3: Identify It

Sedimentary—Hardened sediment with layers of sandy or clay-like stone; gritty feeling; brown or gray; may have fossils and water or wind marks **Yes/No**

Metamorphic—Hard rock with layers of light and dark minerals; curved shape; various colors; may be glittery from mica **Yes/No**

Igneous rock—Solid rock with little texture or layering; mostly black, white and/or gray minerals; may look like granite or like lava **Yes/No**

Test 4: Scratch It

Find out how hard your rock is by trying these tests. Assign the rock a hardness number based on the tests below. Scale Number: _____

Scale	1	2	3	4	5	6	7	8–10
Scratch Test	Leaves a mark when rubbed on the skin	Can be scratched by a fingernail	Can be scratched by a penny	Can be scratched easily by a butter knife	Can be scratched by a butter knife after much effort	Can be scratched with a steel nail but not glass	Can scratch glass	Too hard to be tested on this scale

Test 5: Attract It

Use a magnet to test if your rock contains magnetic material. Describe what happened.

_____

Part 2
Directions: On another sheet of paper, sketch your own diagram of the rock cycle.

Food Chains

Differentiation Strategy

 Choices Board

Standards

- Students will know the organization of simple food chains and food webs.

- TESOL: Students will use English to obtain, process, construct, and provide subject matter information in spoken and written form.

Materials

- lesson resources (pages 108–111)

- pictures of six parts of a food chain (fox.pdf, grass.pdf, hawk.pdf, rabbit.pdf, snake.pdf, sun.pdf)

- glue

- index cards

- books and websites about ecosystems (See page 167.)

- pocket chart or bulletin board

- computer software

- art supplies

- construction paper

Procedures

Preparation Note: Print out photos or illustrations of the parts of a familiar food chain. Glue the pictures onto index cards. You will need a sun, a plant (grass), an herbivore (rabbit), an omnivore (fox), a larger carnivore (snake), and the top predator with no natural enemies (hawk). Make two sets of these pictures.

❶ Display one set of the food-chain pictures, in no particular order, so that the whole class can see them. Then, distribute the other six pictures to six students. *Hint:* This is a great way to get below-grade-level learners and English language learners involved in a whole-class activity. Do not mention food chains or food webs yet. Ask the six students to organize themselves into an order that makes sense to them. When they are ready, have the volunteers stand in order and hold their pictures for everyone to see. Ask the rest of the class to decide if they agree or disagree with the chosen order. Have students explain their opinions and offer alternate suggestions.

❷ If students guess that this lesson is related to food chains, that is a great start. You can assess students' background knowledge of the topic during the follow-up discussion. If students do not bring up the idea of food chains, introduce the concept at this point in the lesson. Explain how food chains work within ecosystems.

★ **English Language Support**—Use the pictures as visual aids to explain the parts of the food chain. Point out that energy comes from the sun, so all food chains start with the sun. Explain that plants use the sun's energy to make their own food. You might wish to introduce vocabulary such as *predator*, *prey*, *herbivore*, *carnivore*, and *omnivore*.

❸ Divide the class into seven heterogeneous groups. Give each group one of the index cards labeled with the following ecosystems—*desert, prairie, pond, ocean, woodland, arctic,* and *rainforest.* Have each group brainstorm animals that live in the ecosystem named on their card. Provide books and websites about ecosystems for students to use as quick references. Have students create simple food chains to share with the class. The food chains must include the ecosystem name and at least one animal for each category—primary producer, primary consumer, secondary consumer, tertiary consumer, quaternary consumer, and top predator.

Food Chains

4 If time allows, have each group present its food chain to the class. If time is limited, have groups display their food chains on desks to create a gallery. The whole class can take a gallery walk to see their classmates' projects.

5 To learn more about food chains, students will complete two additional activities. Assign students a shape based on their readiness levels.

6 Cut apart the *Who Eats Whom? Choices Cards* activity sheets (pages 109–111) and display the cards in a pocket chart or on a bulletin board. Read the activities aloud and explain them. Answer students' questions.

7 Distribute copies of the *Who Eats Whom? Choices Board* activity sheet (page 108). As you pass out the papers, quickly sketch the appropriate shape at the top of each student's sheet. Explain that square (on-grade-level) students will choose a square activity to complete independently and a triangle activity to complete with a friend in their group. Circle (below-grade-level) students will choose a circle activity to complete independently and a square activity to complete with a friend in their group. Triangle (above-grade-level) students will choose two triangle activities to complete. They will complete one independently and one with a friend in their group. Provide students with any needed materials to help them complete the activities.

8 If students finish early, they may complete the Anchor Activity.

Assessment

Evaluate student's activities to be sure that they are working at the appropriate levels and understand the concepts that have been taught.

Activity Levels
▲
Above Grade Level
■
On Grade Level
●
Below Grade Level

Anchor Activity

Have students design a rubric for grading the choices board projects. Provide sample rubrics and a list of your expectations for them to use as references. Another option is to have students design a quiz to assess students' understanding of the lesson.

Name _____

Who Eats Whom? Choices Board

Directions: Choose two activities from the choices board that match the shape assigned to you by your teacher.

Create a board game about producers, consumers, and decomposers. Make sure the action of the game shows the relationships among the three parts. ▢	Research a food chain in the mangrove ecosystem. Discover ideas for preserving the mangrove ecosystems. Design a poster to report your findings. △	Draw and label a food chain that includes you. Your food chain must have at least five links. ◯
Act out a predator/prey relationship in front of the class. Explain how the animals fit into the food chain in their environment. ◯	Create a graphic organizer for a food chain in your environment. Make sure your graphic organizer is neat and colorful. ▢	Research the defining traits of herbivores, omnivores, and carnivores. Combine the traits in an original way to invent a new species of herbivore, omnivore, and carnivore. Create fact cards to introduce the new animals. △
Research two or three food chains that interconnect to form a food web. Use computer software or art supplies to draw and label this food web. △	Draw an outline of each organism in a food chain on a different color sheet of construction paper. Make the first organism the smallest and the top predator the largest. ◯	What happens when one link in a food chain weakens or disappears? Find an example of a food chain that has experienced this. Write a letter from the perspective of the organism that disappeared. ▢
Add your own idea and get your teacher's approval. ▢	Add your own idea and get your teacher's approval. △	Add your own idea and get your teacher's approval. ◯

Name _____

Who Eats Whom? Choices Cards

Directions: Choose two activities to complete.

Research a food chain in the mangrove ecosystem.

Discover ideas for preserving the mangrove ecosystems.

Design a poster to report your findings.

Research the defining traits of herbivores, omnivores, and carnivores.

Combine the traits in an original way to invent a new species of herbivore, omnivore, and carnivore.

Create fact cards to introduce the new animals.

Research two or three food chains that interconnect to form a food web.

Use computer software or art supplies to draw and label this food web.

Add your own idea and get your teacher's approval.

Name _____

Who Eats Whom? Choices Cards

Directions: Choose two activities to complete.

Create a board game about producers, consumers, and decomposers.

Make sure the action of the game shows the relationships among the three parts.

Create a graphic organizer for a food chain in your environment.

Make sure your graphic organizer is neat and colorful.

What happens when one link in a food chain weakens or disappears?

Find an example of a food chain that has experienced this.

Write a letter from the perspective of the organism that disappeared.

Add your own idea and get your teacher's approval.

Name _____

Who Eats Whom? Choices Cards

Directions: Choose two activities to complete.

Draw and label a food chain that includes you. Your food chain must have at least five links.	Draw an outline of each organism in a food chain on a different color sheet of construction paper. Make the first organism the smallest and the top predator the largest.
Act out a predator/prey relationship in front of the class. Explain how the animals fit into the food chain in their environment.	Add your own idea and get your teacher's approval.

Inherited Traits

Differentiation Strategy

 Bloom's Taxonomy

Standards

- Students will know that many characteristics of plants and animals are inherited from its parents, and other characteristics result from an individual's interactions with the environment.

- TESOL: Students will use appropriate learning strategies to construct and apply academic knowledge.

Materials

- lesson resources (pages 114–117)

- family photos (brought from home) or photos of famous families

- large construction paper

- photo-safe tape

Procedures

Preparation Note: Ask students to bring in photos of their family members, especially parents and grandparents. If this is a problem for some students, have them work with partners or have them study the inherited traits of a famous family, such as the First Family or a family of popular actors.

1 Begin the lesson by asking students if anyone has ever told them that they look like one or both of their parents. Allow time for students to share anecdotes. Then, ask students to explain why children usually look like their parents. Ask them to explain why some children might not look like their birth parents.

2 Display the *DNA Graphic Organizer* activity sheet (page 114) and distribute copies to students. Ask them to use the sheet to organize the facts that they will learn during the lesson. Explain that you will model how to complete the organizer as they follow along.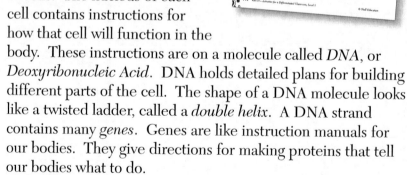

3 Explain that people are made of cells. The nucleus of each cell contains instructions for how that cell will function in the body. These instructions are on a molecule called *DNA*, or *Deoxyribonucleic Acid*. DNA holds detailed plans for building different parts of the cell. The shape of a DNA molecule looks like a twisted ladder, called a *double helix*. A DNA strand contains many *genes*. Genes are like instruction manuals for our bodies. They give directions for making proteins that tell our bodies what to do.

★ **English Language Support**—As you discuss the molecule of DNA and how it relates to inherited traits, use the *DNA Graphic Organizer* (page 114) images as visuals for these learners. Use gestures and point to certain features on the body so that these learners can make sense of the concepts.

Inherited Traits

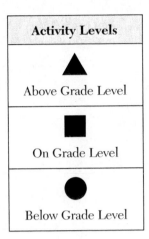

4 Tell students that humans have 25,000 genes. These genes are packed into tiny units called *chromosomes*. Each human cell has 46 chromosomes. One set of 23 chromosomes comes from the mother, and the other set of 23 chromosomes comes from the father. That is how children inherit traits from parents. This passing of traits from parent to child is called *heredity*. Heredity determines *physical traits*, such as hair color, eye color, and height; *behavioral traits*, such as preferences; and *predisposition to medical conditions*, such as diabetes.

5 Explain to students that the focus of today's lesson will be on physical traits passed from parents to children. These are traits that you can see. Have students take out their family photos. Distribute large pieces of construction paper and photo-safe tape. Have students tape the photos to the paper with the oldest relatives at the top and the youngest relatives at the bottom of the page.

6 Ask students to examine the family photos. Have them identify at least three physical traits that are shared by their family members, such as hair color, hair texture, skin color, eye color, and height. Tell them to label the photos with information about the subject's physical traits. Then, ask them to share observations about heredity.

7 Students will learn more about inherited traits. Distribute copies of the *Questions About Heredity* activity sheets (pages 115–117) to students based on their readiness levels.

8 Provide students with enough time to complete the activity sheets and then review the concepts as a whole class.

9 If students finish early, they may complete the Anchor Activity.

Assessment

Have students complete an exit slip summarizing their learning. Evaluate students' comments to ensure that lesson objectives were met.

Activity Levels
▲
Above Grade Level
■
On Grade Level
●
Below Grade Level

Anchor Activity

Have students research the history of human genetics. Challenge them to find out when DNA was discovered, who discovered it, and how it was discovered. In addition, have students find out what unknowns remain in the field of genetic research today.

Name _____

DNA Graphic Organizer

Directions: As you learn facts about DNA and inherited traits, write them on the lines below.

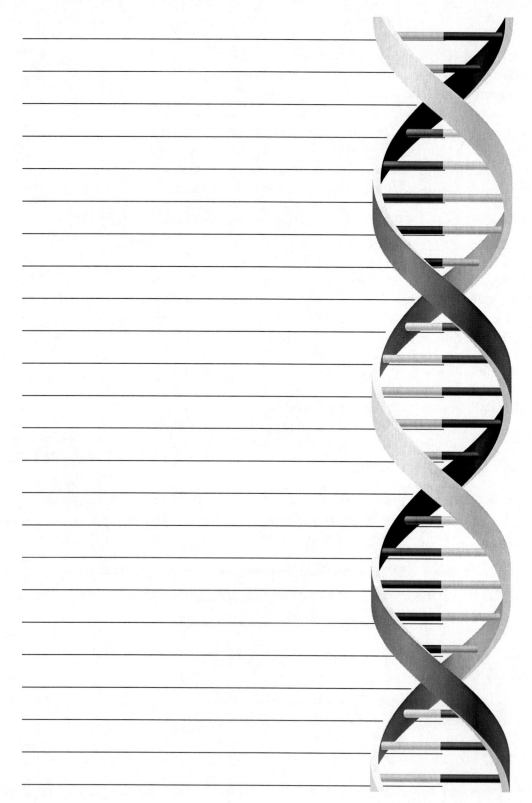

© *Shell Education*

Name _____

Questions About Heredity

Directions: Answer the questions about heredity. Some questions might require further research on the topic.

Evaluating: Do you think genetics, the study of heredity, is an important field of research? Defend your answer.

_____

_____

_____

_____

_____

Creating: Why do children born to the same parents look different? Read more about dominant and recessive genes. Find out exactly how children inherit physical traits. Then, create a fictional family. In the box below, draw and color pictures of a man and a woman that show physical traits such as hair, eye, and skin color; hair texture; height; and facial features. List at least six physical traits for each person. Then, use what you know about heredity and dominant and recessive genes to design two children for the couple. Draw and color the kids. Then, list six physical traits that they inherited. On another sheet of paper, diagram how they inherited their traits.

Name _____

Directions: Answer the questions about heredity.

Applying: Do you understand genetics well enough to explain the basics to a friend? Write a kid-friendly explanation of heredity on the lines below. Use simple, clear words to explain the basics. Define vocabulary words such as *DNA, genes, chromosomes,* and *heredity* as simply as possible.

_____

_____

_____

_____

_____

_____

_____

_____

Analyzing: Why do you look the way you look? Study family photos and ask questions about the physical traits of your parents and grandparents. Make a list of five of your own physical traits, such as eye color, hair color, and height. Trace these inherited traits back to your grandparents. Draw a diagram that explains exactly how you inherited your traits.

_____

_____

Name _____

Questions About Heredity

Directions: Answer the questions about heredity.

Understanding: Do you understand the new words in the lesson? Write a definition in your own words for each of the words below.

DNA _____

_____

gene _____

_____

chromosome _____

_____

physical trait _____

_____

heredity _____

_____

Applying: How would you explain the way children inherit their parents' traits? Write a kid-friendly description of this process on the lines below. Use simple, clear words to explain the basics. Include at least three of the vocabulary words listed above.

_____

_____

_____

_____

_____

_____

_____

_____

_____

_____

_____

_____

Animal Adaptations

Differentiation Strategy

 Tiered Graphic Organizers

Standards

• Students will know basic ideas related to biological evolution.

• TESOL: Students will use appropriate learning strategies to construct and apply academic knowledge.

Materials

• lesson resources (pages 120–123)

• photos of animals with adaptations

• books and websites about animal adaptations *(See page 167.)*

Procedures

1 Begin the lesson by showing photos of skunks, giraffes, camels, turtles, zebras, polar bears, chameleons, and any other animals with interesting adaptations. Do not mention adaptations yet. Ask students to think about what these animals have in common. Have them think-pair-share their ideas.

2 Discuss students' responses as a whole class. If students need a hint, narrow the question by asking what a skunk's spray and a chameleon's ability to change color have in common. The correct answer is that they are both adaptations that help the animals to protect themselves.

3 Write the word *adaptation* on the board. Gauge students' prior knowledge by asking them to indicate familiarity with the word with a "thumbs up" or "thumbs down" sign. Encourage students to keep their fists close to their chests so as not to show the whole class their response. This will allow students to respond honestly without embarrassment.

4 Ask a volunteer who signaled "thumbs up" to explain adaptation and give examples. After a brief discussion, write this definition on the board: *A trait that enables an organism to survive in its environment.*

5 Assign homogeneous partners for an activity about animal adaptations. Distribute copies of the *Rank the Animal Adaptations* activity sheet (page 120) to students. Have the above-grade-level students read the directions and definitions independently. Read the directions and definitions aloud to the on-grade-level and below-grade-level students. Provide time for pairs to complete the activity in class. Then, review responses as a whole class. To some extent, this is an opinion activity, but *Animal Planet*™ has ranked the Top 10 Animal Adaptations (see **www.animal.discovery.com**).

Animal Adaptations

6 Distribute copies of the *Animal Adaptations* activity sheets (pages 121–123) to students based on their readiness levels. Students will research animal adaptations and record their findings on the graphic organizers. Provide books and websites for students to use for research.

★ **English Language Support**—Help these students succeed at research by choosing simple, easy-to-read materials with many photos, illustrations, and other graphic elements. Websites with video and audio clips would be especially beneficial to these learners.

7 After students have completed their graphic organizers, have them share their findings with the class.

8 If students finish early, they may complete the Anchor Activity.

Activity Levels
▲
Above Grade Level
■
On Grade Level
●
Below Grade Level

Assessment

Evaluate students' graphic organizers to be sure that they are working at the appropriate levels and understand the concepts that have been taught. Make adjustments, as needed, especially for future assignments.

Anchor Activity

Have students each write and illustrate a picture book about animal adaptations. The book should take the form of a narrative story with animals as the main characters. The story should have a setting and a plot. Ask students to think about an audience of preschool children as they write their stories.

Name _____

Rank the Animal Adaptations

Directions: Read about each animal adaptation below. Think about the importance and usefulness of each adaptation. Then, rank the adaptations from the least important (10) to the most important (1). Write your rank on the line.

_____ **appearing larger**—Many animals have ways of making themselves look larger to scare off predators.

_____ **camouflage**—Many animals are born with coloring that allows them to blend in to their environments. This helps them hide from predators. Other species have the amazing ability to change their appearance to match their surroundings.

_____ **communal living**—Living together in groups helps many species survive by providing safety in numbers. The animal communities also share the work of finding food and caring for the young.

_____ **flight**—The ability to fly helps some animals move quickly from place to place. It allows them to escape predators and find resources that are out of reach for other species.

_____ **hair**—Mammals depend on hair to protect them from the elements, such as extreme cold.

_____ **hibernation**—Many animals avoid frigid weather and scarce resources by falling into a deep sleep for the winter.

_____ **migration**—Some animals temporarily leave an environment with harsh weather to move to a more comfortable climate where food is plentiful.

_____ **nest parasitism**—Some birds lay their eggs in the nests of another species. The adoptive mother feeds and cares for the orphans. Because the orphans are usually larger and more aggressive than their nest mates, they win the fight for food. Some orphan babies will even push other eggs and baby birds out of the nest to ensure their own survival.

_____ **playing dead**—In the face of danger, some animals fall to the ground and lie motionless. Their tongues hang out of their mouths and their eyes glaze over. They look and feel dead. Predators quickly lose interest because long-dead prey makes a bad meal.

_____ **resource conservation**—Some animals who live in environments where resources are limited have developed ways to store fat and water for long periods of time.

Challenge: If time allows, list animals that can make each adaptation.

Name _____

Animal Adaptations

Part 1 Directions: Study three different biomes. Learn about how the animals in each biome have adapted to their environments. Design a graphic organizer to organize your findings. Remember, graphic organizers can take many different forms, such as charts, webs, diagrams, and trees. Use the box below for your work.

Part 2 Directions: Now, mix up your findings. What adaptations would the animals on your organizer need if they moved to a different biome? How would they look? How would they act? On another sheet of paper, draw pictures of three animals as you imagine they would look if they adapted to new environments. Write captions that explain their adaptations.

Name _____

Animal Adaptations

Directions: Research the adaptations of at least five different species. Complete the graphic organizer below.

Animal	Habitat	Adaptation(s)	Type of Adaptation	Reason for Adaptation

1. What is the most interesting animal adaptation on your chart? Explain your opinion.

_____

_____

2. What is the most important animal adaptation on your chart? Explain your opinion.

_____

_____

_____

3. Describe one pattern or trend that you see on your chart.

_____

_____

Name _____

Animal Adaptations

Directions: The *Rank the Animal Adaptations* activity sheet described 10 different ways that animals adapt. Reread the sheet carefully. Research to find at least one example of an animal with each adaptation. On the chart below, list the animal name and a description of the adaptation.

Type of Adaptation (from *Rank the Animal Adaptations*)	Animal(s)	Describe the Adaptation(s)
appearing larger		
camouflage		
communal living		
flight		
hair		
hibernation		
migration		
nest parasitism		
playing dead		
resource conservation		

Forces and Motion

Differentiation Strategy

 Menu of Options

Standards

- Students will know that when a force is applied to an object, the object either speeds up, slows down, or goes in a different direction.

- TESOL: Students will use English to obtain, process, construct, and provide subject matter information in spoken and written form.

Materials

- lesson resources (pages 126–129)

- video clips of Newton's laws of motion and astronaut on the moon (*See page 167.*)

- *menu of options materials:* stopwatch, meterstick, toy cars and ramps, Internet, printer, glue, poster board, digital camera, slide show software, art supplies, marbles, index cards, bouncy ball, paper clip

Procedures

❶ Begin the lesson by showing video clips or photos of Newton's three laws of motion in action. The first time you show the clips, simply push play without any explanation or introduction. You might need to mute the sound if the video clip explains the forces of motion. For the second showing, ask students to pay careful attention. Then, pause before each clip to tell students, *"This clip shows Newton's first (second, third) law of motion."* Do not explain the laws at this point.

❷ Divide the class into three heterogeneous groups. Randomly assign each group one of the laws of motion. Based only on what they remember from the video clips, have students try to guess the definition of their assigned law of motion. Have them write their guesses on notebook paper.

❸ Before collecting the guesses, show the video clips a third time. Remind students to pay careful attention to the video clip that shows their group's law in action. Then, allow students to revise their guesses, as needed.

❹ Read each guess aloud as you play the corresponding video clip. As a whole class, discuss the video clips and the guesses.

❺ Display the correct definitions of Newton's laws of motion, explain them, and provide examples.

Newton's First Law—An object at rest tends to stay at rest, and an object in motion tends to stay in motion unless a force acts upon that object. This is also called *inertia*.

Newton's Second Law—The acceleration of an object depends on the mass of an object and amount of force applied. The force of an object is equal to its mass times its acceleration.

Newton's Third Law—Every action has an equal and opposite reaction.

Forces and Motion

6 Distribute copies of the *Forces and Motion Menu of Options* activity sheets (pages 126–127) to students. Explain to students that they will choose activities from the menu to learn more about forces and motion. Decide ahead of time how many points students need to complete from the menu, and set a due date for the projects. Read each activity aloud and answer any questions that students may have.

7 Distribute the *Forces and Motion Project Action Plan* activity sheet (page 128) to students to help them plan their activities.

★ **English Language Support**—Use this time to meet with these students to make sure that they choose projects at their readiness levels. Reread the activity directions and show students sample projects so they can see what is expected. If necessary, modify the activities to meet individual needs. Help students complete their action plans.

8 Provide students with any needed materials to help them complete the activities. Allow students time to complete their menu of options projects.

9 If students finish early, they may complete the Anchor Activity.

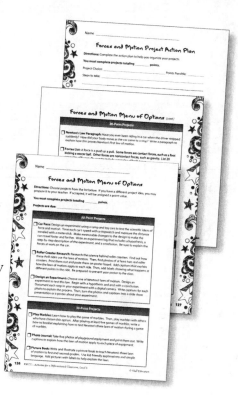

Assessment

To assess what students have learned, distribute copies of *Forces and Motion Assessment* activity sheet (page 129).

Anchor Activity

Have students create their own videos or skits that show all three of Newton's laws. They can tape the performances or perform them live for the class.

Name _____

Forces and Motion Menu of Options

Directions: Choose projects from the list below. If you have a different project idea, you may propose it to your teacher. If accepted, it will be assigned a point value.

You must complete projects totaling _____ points.

Projects are due: _____

50-Point Projects

☐ **Car Race:** Design an experiment using a ramp and toy cars to test the scientific ideas of force and motion. Time each car's speed with a stopwatch and measure the distance traveled with a meterstick. Make measurable changes to the design to make the cars travel faster and farther. Write an experiment log that includes a hypothesis, a step-by-step description of the experiment, and a conclusion. Be sure to explain the forces at work on the car.

☐ **Roller Coaster Research:** Research the science behind roller coasters. Find out how these thrill rides use the laws of motion. Then, find photos of at least two real roller coasters. Print them out and paste them on poster board. Add captions that explain how the laws of motion apply to each ride. Then, add labels showing what happens at different points in the ride. Be prepared to present your poster to the class.

☐ **Design an Experiment:** Choose one of Newton's laws of motion. Design an experiment to test this law. Begin with a hypothesis and end with a conclusion. Document each step in your experiment with a digital camera. Write captions for each photo to explain the process. Then, turn the photos and captions into a slide show presentation or a poster about your experiment.

30-Point Projects

☐ **Play Marbles:** Learn how to play the game of marbles. Then, play marbles with others who have chosen this option. After playing at least five games of marbles, write a how-to booklet explaining how to test Newton's three laws of motion during a game of marbles.

☐ **Photo Journal:** Take five photos of playground equipment and print them out. Write captions to explain how the laws of motion apply to each piece of equipment.

☐ **Picture Book:** Write and illustrate a picture book to teach Newton's three laws of motion to first and second graders. Use kid-friendly explanations and simple language. Add pictures with labels to help explain the laws.

Forces and Motion Menu of Options *(cont.)*

20-Point Projects

☐ **Newton's Law Paragraph:** Have you ever been riding in a car when the driver stopped suddenly? How did your body move as the car came to a stop? Write a paragraph to explain how this proves Newton's first law of motion.

☐ **Forces List:** A force is a push or a pull. Some forces are contact forces, such as a foot kicking a soccer ball. Other forces are noncontact forces, such as gravity. List 20 examples of forces. Be sure to include examples of both types.

10-Point Projects

☐ **Forces Vocabulary:** The terms *motion, force, inertia,* and *reaction* are key to understanding forces and motion. For each of the vocabulary words, divide an index card into four quadrants. In one quadrant, write a definition. In the second quadrant, write the characteristics of the term. In the third quadrant, list examples. In the fourth quadrant, list nonexamples.

☐ **Gravity Comic Strip:** If you drop a marble, a bouncy ball, and a paper clip from the top of a slide, which will land first? Why? Conduct an experiment with these items. Draw a comic strip to explain the answer.

☐ **Watch a Video:** Watch a video clip online of an astronaut walking on the moon. Write a paragraph describing what you see in scientific terms.

Student-Proposed Projects

☐ _____
_____
_____

☐ _____
_____
_____

Name _____

Forces and Motion Project Action Plan

Directions: Complete the action plan to help you organize your projects.

You must complete projects totaling _____ points.

Project Choice: _____ Points Possible: _____

Steps to take: _____

_____

_____

Project Choice: _____ Points Possible: _____

Steps to take: _____

_____

_____

Project Choice: _____ Points Possible: _____

Steps to take: _____

_____

_____

Project Choice: _____ Points Possible: _____

Steps to take: _____

_____

_____

Project Choice: _____ Points Possible: _____

Steps to take: _____

_____

_____

Add the points from each project choice above. Total points possible: _____

Projects are due: _____

Name _____

Forces and Motion Assessment

Directions: See if you can figure out which of Newton's laws goes with each picture.

1. This scene shows a batter hitting a baseball. The harder he hits, the farther the ball will go. What law of motion does this represent? What does this law of motion say?

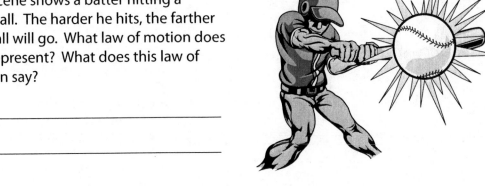

_____

_____

_____

_____

2. This scene shows kids jumping on a trampoline. When they push against the trampoline, the trampoline pushes back and causes them to jump in the air. What law of motion does this represent? What does this law of motion say?

_____

_____

_____

_____

3. This scene shows two cars crashing and the passengers flying out of the cars. What law of motion does this represent? What does this law of motion say?

_____

_____

_____

_____

Colonial America

Differentiation Strategy

☑ **Menu of Options**

Standards

• Students will understand the factors that shaped the economic system in the American colonies.

• TESOL: Students will use English to obtain, process, construct, and provide subject matter information in spoken and written form.

Materials

• lesson resources (pages 132–135)

• chart paper and markers

• books and websites on Colonial America and colonists *(See page 167.)*

• sticky notes

• index cards

• audio recorder

• art supplies

• camera

Procedures

Note: The activity in this lesson will work best at the end of a unit on Colonial America. It also can be used as an assessment to see what students have learned.

★ **English Language Support**—Post Colonial America vocabulary terms with both definitions and pictures. Classwide conversations and discussions will be critical for better understanding.

❶ Distribute copies of the *Colonists in America* activity sheet (page 132) to students. Also, display this graphic organizer on the board or on chart paper to collect students' answers.

❷ Divide the class into four groups (one group for each country listed) or divide the class into eight groups (two groups for each country listed). Assign each group one of the following countries: Spain, France, England, or the Netherlands. Provide time for students to research the information needed to fill in their specific part of the graphic organizer. Allow students to use the Internet, textbooks, and the additional books that you have provided on Colonial America.

❸ Once students have collected the information, have them add the information that they found by recording it on sticky notes or index cards and placing them on the board in the correct parts of the graphic organizer. Each group can report to the class its findings about the country it was assigned.

❹ While each group reports its findings, the rest of the students should fill in their graphic organizers with the information that is being reported. All students should have completed graphic organizers after every group has presented.

Colonial America

❺ Explain to students that they will show you what they have learned by completing activities found on a menu of options. First, decide how many points you want students to earn. Then, distribute copies of the *Colonial America Review Menu of Options* activity sheets (pages 133–134) to students and go over all the activities. Answer any questions that students might have and set a due date for projects.

★ **English Language Support**—Make an audio recording of the menu of options so that students can listen to it repeatedly. Make adjustments to their assignments, allowing students to verbally explain, act out, or make audio recordings of their work instead of turning in written work.

❻ Explain to students that they will plan their activities by filling in the *Colonial America Review Project Planning Guide* activity sheet (page 135) and turning it in to you before beginning their projects. This way, you know which activities each student plans to complete and you can provide individualized support. Provide students with any needed materials to help them complete the activities.

❼ If students finish early, they may complete the Anchor Activity.

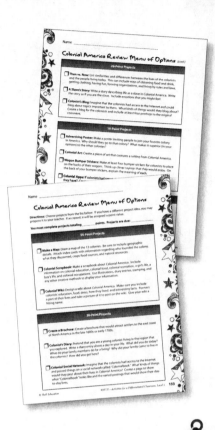

Assessment

Evaluate students' work from their menu of options to be sure that they understand the concepts that have been taught. Meet with small groups of struggling students to reteach any difficult concepts or ideas.

Anchor Activity

Have students research the kinds of foods that colonists enjoyed the most. Have students make a recipe book with at least four recipes, and then prepare one item to bring in to class to share. Have students label the ingredients included in any food that they bring to alert others who may have food allergies.

Name _____

Colonists in America

Directions: Fill in your part of the graphic organizer below. As your classmates report their information, fill in the rest of the information that is needed.

Country	Name of Colony	Location	Reason for Settlement
Spain			
France			
England			
Netherlands			

Name _____

Colonial America Review Menu of Options

Directions: Choose projects from the list below. If you have a different project idea, you may propose it to your teacher. If accepted, it will be assigned a point value.

You must complete projects totaling _____ points. Projects are due: _____

50-Point Projects

☐ **Make a Map:** Draw a map of the 13 colonies. Be sure to include geographic details. Attach index cards with information regarding who founded the colony, what they discovered, crops/food sources, and natural resources.

☐ **Colonial Scrapbook:** Make a scrapbook about Colonial America. Include information on colonial education, colonial food, colonial recreation, a girl's life, a boy's life, and colonial occupations. Use illustrations, diary entries, stamping, and any other creative methods to display your information.

☐ **Colonial Wiki:** Design a wiki about Colonial America. Make sure you include colonists' education, food, dress, how they lived, and interesting facts. Reenact a part of their lives and take a picture of it to post on the wiki. Give your wiki a fitting name.

30-Point Projects

☐ **Create a Brochure:** Create a brochure that would attract settlers to the east coast of North America in the late 1600s or early 1700s.

☐ **Colonist's Diary:** Pretend that you are a young colonist living in the region that you explored. Write a diary entry about a day in your life. What did you do today? What do your family members do for a living? Why did your family come to live in the colonies? How did you get here?

☐ **Colonial Social Network:** Imagine that the colonists had access to the Internet and posted things on a social network called "Colonialbook." What kinds of things would they post about their lives in Colonial America? Create a page to show what "Colonialbook" looks like and the varied postings that would show their day-to-day lives.

Name _____

Colonial America Review Menu of Options *(cont.)*

20-Point Projects

☐ **Then vs. Now:** List similarities and differences between the lives of the colonists and the people living today. This can include ways of obtaining food and drink, getting clothing, having fun, forming organizations, and living by rules and laws.

☐ **A Slave's Story:** Write a story describing life as a slave in Colonial America. Write the story as if you are the slave. Include emotions that you might feel.

☐ **Colonist's Blog:** Imagine that the colonists had access to the Internet and could blog about topics important to them. What kinds of things would they blog about? Create a blog for the colonists and include at least four postings to the original comment.

10-Point Projects

☐ **Advertising Poster:** Make a poster inviting people to join your favorite colony in America. Why should they go to that colony? What makes it superior (in your opinion) to the other colonies?

☐ **Colonial Art:** Create a piece of art that captures a setting from Colonial America.

☐ **Wagon Bumper Stickers:** Make at least four bumper stickers for colonists to place on the backs of their wagons. Think up clever sayings that they would enjoy. On the back of your bumper stickers, explain the meaning of each.

☐ **Colonial Apps:** If colonists had smart phones, what kinds of applications would they have? Create at least four apps that would be useful for the colonists.

Student-Proposed Projects

☐ _____

_____

_____

☐ _____

_____

_____

Name _____

Colonial America Review
Project Planning Guide

Directions: Choose projects from the menu of options (or create and submit your own for your teachers' approval) and write them in the column below their point value. Use extra space to list the steps that you will need to take to complete the projects.

You must complete enough projects to earn _____ points.

Projects are due: _____

Project Choices

50 Points	30 Points	20 Points	10 Points	Alternative Choice

Total Project Points: _____

Revolutionary Social Networking

Differentiation Strategy

 Tiered Graphic Organizers

Standards

- Students will understand the social, political, and economic effects of the American revolutionary victory on different groups.

- TESOL: Students will use English to obtain, process, construct, and provide subject matter information in spoken and written form.

Materials

- lesson resources (pages 138–141)

- books, websites, and resources about the American Revolution (See page 167.)

- timer

- bulletin board

Procedures

❶ Begin the lesson by having students find partners for a scavenger hunt. Explain to students that you will give them between five and 10 minutes to list as many important people who were involved in the American Revolution as they can. They may use the Internet, textbooks, and other available resources on the American Revolution. If possible, arrange for other classes or office staff to assist your students in this scavenger hunt. Set a timer and let students search.

❷ When the timer goes off, bring the class together to share their lists. Make a master list on the board of these important people.

❸ Tell students that they will be choosing one person from the American Revolution to research. After they find information about this person, they will create a social network page for this famous person.

Important People of the American Revolution

Margaret Corbin, Paul Revere, Elizabeth Freeman, Deborah Sampson, Molly Pitcher, Benedict Arnold, John Paul Jones, Nathan Hale, George Washington, John Hancock, Phillis Wheatley, Thomas Jefferson, Benjamin Franklin, Samuel Adams, John Adams, Edward Braddock, King George III, Patrick Henry

---

❹ Distribute copies of the *Revolutionary Social Network Example* activity sheet (page 138) to students. Review this example with students to engage them in the assignment. Explain that they will create a page like this for someone who lived during the American Revolution. Their page may contain some or all of the elements that they see on this sample, and can also include additional information.

Revolutionary Social Networking

5 First, students must each do some research on their famous person and record information on a graphic organizer. Distribute copies of the *Revolutionary Book Graphic Organizer* activity sheets (pages 139–141) to students based on readiness levels. Have students read the directions and begin their research.

★ **English Language Support**—Have your English language learners complete the on-grade-level graphic organizer because it involves minimal writing. If students are not able to write the captions and information on that page, have them present it to you orally.

6 Meet with your below-grade-level students and read the directions aloud. Model how to find important information about these famous people.

7 After all students have completed their graphic organizers, have them present their information to the class. Post these on a Revolutionary Book bulletin board for everyone to enjoy.

8 If students finish early, they may complete the Anchor Activity.

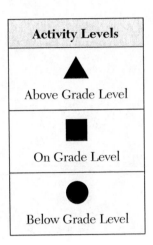

Activity Levels
▲
Above Grade Level
■
On Grade Level
●
Below Grade Level

Assessment

Grade students' activity sheets based on completeness and creativity. You may wish to develop rubrics with the class so that students understand how they will be evaluated.

Anchor Activity

Have students create interesting clubs that many of the Revolutionary figures would have wanted to join. They can make a list of these for the class and post them on a bulletin board.

Revolutionary Social Network Example

Directions: Use this sample to see what a social networking site looks like.

Information

Sex: Male

Birthday: February 22, 1732

Looking for: Friends, Networking

Location: Tent, planning battles during the American Revolution

Hometown: Westmoreland County, Virginia

Political Views: Go Yanks!

Friends

George Washington

About Me

Bio: I was born in Virginia. My father died when I was 11, and since I was the oldest of 6 children, I ended up with a lot of responsibility. I was really good at math and earned enough money as a surveyor to start buying my own land. My older half-brother also helped me make my way in the world by introducing me to important people. I inherited Mount Vernon from my half-brother when he died. In 1752, I was put in charge of Virginia's military even though I hadn't been a soldier before; talk about an introduction! In 1759, I resigned from the military and went home to Mount Vernon. I married Martha Custis and helped raise her two young children. In 1759, I was also elected to the House of Burgesses—part of the government— and kept being elected until 1774. Now that the colonies have declared independence from King George III of England, I'm back in the military, in charge of soldiers and out here in the middle of the American Revolution.

George Washington Please remind me why we are out here again. I'm getting a bit tired of being at war. It seems the war will never end and our soldiers grow tired. Who can blame them? In the summer it is stifling hot and mosquitoes as big as chickens are all over. In the winter it is freezing and miserable. It would be nice if Ben could use some of his lightning experiments to invent something useful…instead of just flying kites during storms.

Paul Revere Didn't you listen? Do I need to say it again? THE BRITISH ARE COMING!!! What did you think I meant? They were coming for dinner? Apparently, they came to stay awhile and it will be some time before we can announce that they are leaving. Keep your chin up and be glad they wear those nice red coats. I hear the British wardrobe doesn't blend into the forest all that well.

John Hancock So, you're not too happy I signed my name as large as I did? It seems King George indeed read the Declaration and got the message. Well, it can't be undone now. Hang in there and keep fighting. I hear good things about Yorktown.

Benjamin Franklin Inventing the lightning rod wasn't enough for you? Feel free to fly a kite in the middle of a storm any time you want. You should come on over to France! People are very friendly and you can't beat brie and baguette for lunch!

Martha Washington Sorry you are having a rough day, Dear. Just remember the British are nothing compared to what I will say if you decide to run for office when this war is over. Come home to Virginia!

Name _____

RevolutionaryBook Graphic Organizer

Directions: Fill in the graphic organizer below to show what you have learned about the person you researched. On the Wall tab, be sure to write posts that show what is on this person's mind and what he or she has been doing.

Name: _____

Wall

Photo of Me

Information

_____

_____

_____

_____

Friends

Name _____

RevolutionaryBook Graphic Organizer

Directions: Fill in the graphic organizer below to show what you have learned about the person you researched. On the Photos tab, be sure to draw pictures, name the albums, and post comments that show what is on this person's mind and what he or she has been doing.

Name: _____

Photo of Me

Photos

Album Name

Album Name

Information

_____

_____

_____

_____

Comments

_____

_____

_____

Comments

_____

_____

_____

Album Name

Album Name

_____

_____

Comments

_____

_____

Comments

_____

_____

Friends

_____

Name _____

RevolutionaryBook Graphic Organizer

Directions: Fill in the graphic organizer below to show what you have learned about the person you researched.

Name: _____

Info

About Me

Photo of Me

Information

_____

_____

_____

_____

Basic Information

Birthday: _____

Residence: _____

Political Views: _____

Education: _____

Employer/Work: _____

One Big Accomplishment: _____

_____

Likes and Interests

Activities: _____

_____

_____

Other: _____

Contact Information

Friends

_____

Declaration of Independence

Social Studies

Differentiation Strategy

 Choices Board

Standards

- Students will understand the major ideas in the Declaration of Independence, their sources, and how they became unifying ideas of American democracy.

- TESOL: Students will use English to obtain, process, construct, and provide subject matter information in spoken and written form.

Materials

- lesson resources (pages 144–147)

- art supplies

Procedures

1 Begin by asking students what they know about the Declaration of Independence. Allow them to share their ideas aloud. Ask students if they know any details about what is written in the famous document.

2 Distribute copies of the *Analyzing the Declaration of Independence* activity sheet (page 144) to students.

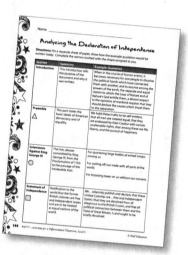

3 Use the Preamble section in the first row to model how to translate its language into modern English. This should not be a line-by-line translation but rather a general summary of what is being said. You may use the text in the box below:

> When a group of people no longer wants to have political ties to another group, they should say why they want to separate.

4 Students can either copy what you have written in the last box or write their own translation.

5 Place students in homogeneous pairs. Assign each pair a shape based on their readiness levels. Have each pair translate the row on the activity sheet that corresponds to their assigned shape. The rows have been differentiated according to difficulty.

★ **English Language Support**—Pair English language learners with language-proficient students. Provide vocabulary support for unfamiliar terms during the translation.

6 After students have completed their translations, have volunteers from each level share their translations with the class. Students should use that information to fill in the rest of their activity sheets.

Declaration of Independence

7 Distribute copies of the *Declaration of Independence Choices Board* (page 145) to students. Assign students shapes based on their readiness levels. Read the activities aloud, and answer any questions that students may have. Explain to students that they will choose two activities to complete that match their assigned shape.

8 Distribute copies of the *Declaration of Independence Project Planning Guide* activity sheet (page 146) to students. Have students write their project choices on this sheet and turn it in to you.

9 Provide students with art supplies to help them complete the activities. Allow time in class for students to complete their work.

10 If students finish early, they may complete the Anchor Activity.

Assessment

Use the *Declaration of Independence Rubric* (page 147) to assess students' projects. You will need a separate rubric for each project that students complete. Be sure to show this rubric to students before they begin working so that they understand how they will be assessed.

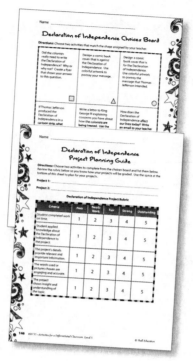

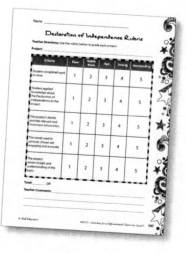

Activity Levels
▲
Above Grade Level
■
On Grade Level
●
Below Grade Level

Anchor Activity

Have students look at another historic document, such as the United States Constitution or the Texas Declaration of Independence, and translate the first paragraph of those documents into modern English.

Name _____

Analyzing the Declaration of Independence

Directions: On a separate sheet of paper, show how the example quotation would be written today. Complete the section marked with the shape assigned to you.

Section	Summary	Example Quotation
Introduction	This introduction tells the purpose of the document and why it was written.	When in the course of human events, it becomes necessary for one people to dissolve the political bands which have connected them with another, and to assume among the powers of the earth, the separate and equal station to which the Laws of Nature and of Nature's God entitle them, a decent respect to the opinions of mankind requires that they should declare the causes which impel them to the separation.
Preamble △	This part states the basic ideals of American democracy and of equality.	We hold these truths to be self-evident, that all men are created equal, that they are endowed by their Creator with certain unalienable rights, that among these are life, liberty, and the pursuit of happiness.
Grievances Against King George III ◯	This lists abuses committed by King George III, from the Proclamation of 1763 to the passage of the Intolerable Acts.	For quartering large bodies of armed troops among us. For cutting off our trade with all parts of the world. For imposing taxes on us without our consent.
Statement of Independence ▢	Notification to the world that the former British colonies are free and independent states and are to be treated as equal nations of the world.	We…solemnly publish and declare, that these United Colonies are…free and Independent States; that they are absolved from all allegiance to the British Crown, and that all political connection between them and the State of Great Britain, is and ought to be totally dissolved.

Name _____

Declaration of Independence Choices Board

Directions: Choose two activities that match the shape assigned by your teacher.

Did the colonists really need to write the Declaration of Independence? Why or why not? Create a flyer that shows your answer to this question. ☐	Design a comic book cover that is *against* the Declaration of Independence. Use colorful artwork to portray your message. △	Design a comic book cover that is *for* the Declaration of Independence. Use colorful artwork to portray the message that Thomas Jefferson intended. ○
If Thomas Jefferson produced the Declaration of Independence in a cartoon strip, what would it look like? Create a six-frame cartoon that explains the Declaration of Independence. ○	Write a letter to King George III explaining concerns you have about how the colonists are being treated. Use the information from the declaration to help you. ☐	How does the Declaration of Independence affect our lives today? Write an email to your teacher with a response that is at least three paragraphs in length. △
Imagine that you are King George III and are reading the Declaration of Independence for the first time. What do you think? How will you respond? Write a response to the colonists about this document. △	Make a T-chart to show the causes and effects of the Declaration of Independence. Show three causes and three effects. You should explain the reasons why the colonists declared independence. **(Hint:** *Use the Declaration of Independence to help you.)* ○	If you had the chance to write the Preamble to the Declaration of Independence, what would it say? Create a text that shows your answer. ☐

Name _____

Declaration of Independence Project Planning Guide

Directions: Choose two activities to complete from the choices board and list them below. Review the rubric below so you know how your projects will be graded. Use the space at the bottom of this sheet to plan for your projects.

Project 1: _____

Project 2: _____

Declaration of Independence Project Rubric

Criteria	Poor	Needs Work	Fair	Strong	Outstanding
Student completed work on time.	1	2	3	4	5
Student applied knowledge about the Declaration of Independence to the project.	1	2	3	4	5
The project's details provide relevant and important information.	1	2	3	4	5
The words used or pictures chosen are engaging and accurate.	1	2	3	4	5
The project shows insight and understanding of the topic.	1	2	3	4	5

Name _____

Declaration of Independence Rubric

Teacher Directions: Use the rubric below to grade each project.

Project: _____

Criteria	Poor	Needs Work	Fair	Strong	Outstanding
Student completed work on time.	1	2	3	4	5
Student applied knowledge about the Declaration of Independence to the project.	1	2	3	4	5
The project's details provide relevant and important information.	1	2	3	4	5
The words used or pictures chosen are engaging and accurate.	1	2	3	4	5
The project shows insight and understanding of the topic.	1	2	3	4	5

Total: _____ /25

Teacher Comments: _____

_____

_____

Westward Expansion

Differentiation Strategy

 Leveled Learning Contracts

Standards

- Students will understand elements of early western migration.

- TESOL: Students will use English to obtain, process, construct, and provide subject matter information in spoken and written form.

Materials

- lesson resources (pages 150–153)

- scissors

- books and websites on westward expansion (See page 167.)

- index cards

- art supplies

- video camera

- shoe boxes

Procedures

Note: This learning contract is best used at the middle or end of a unit on westward expansion. However, it can be distributed at the beginning of the unit and turned in at the end.

Preparation Note: Before class begins, make a copy of the *Westward Expansion Game Cards* (page 150) and cut the cards apart.

❶ Distribute the *Westward Expansion Game Cards* (page 150) to 16 student volunteers. (Partner students or make two copies of the cards to allow the entire class to participate.) Explain to students that some cards have terms and others have the terms' definitions. Tell students to hold their game cards in front of them so that others can see them. Have students walk around the class to find the matches to their cards.

★ **English Language Support**—Be sure to partner these learners with language-proficient students during this activity. They should not work alone. You can also make a copy of the cards for these learners and go through this exercise with them in a small group.

❷ Give students a minute or two to find the match to their card, and then stand next to that person, elbow to elbow. Pairs will then take turns explaining their term and definition to the class.

❸ Repeat this activity, but tell students that they must take a different term or definition.

Westward Expansion

4 Distribute copies of the *Westward Expansion Learning Contract* activity sheets (pages 151–153) to students based on their readiness levels.

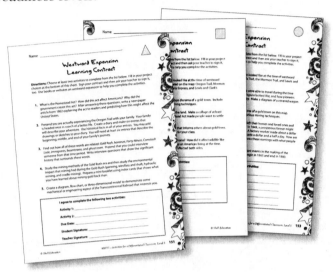

Activity Levels
▲
Above Grade Level
■
On Grade Level
●
Below Grade Level

5 Read the directions to the class and have students review the choices on their contracts. Ask students to select two activities to complete and to fill in their choices on their contracts. Assign a due date for the activities and have students write it on their contracts. Have students sign their contracts at the bottom and then ask you to review and sign it, as well. Provide students with any needed materials to help them complete the activities.

6 Provide independent work time for students to complete their activities in class. This time can offer an excellent opportunity to work with small groups of students on preteaching, reteaching, or extending unit lessons. Or, assign the contract activities as homework.

7 If students finish early, they may complete the Anchor Activity.

Assessment

Evaluate students' projects to determine whether the lesson objectives were met. You may wish to develop a criteria chart or rubric with the students before they begin work so that they understand how they will be assessed.

Anchor Activity

Have students extend their learning to find out more about American Indians and how westward expansion affected their lives. Students can present their findings as a poster, a report, pictures, or cartoons.

Westward Expansion Game Cards

Directions: Cut out the cards below and distribute a card to each student.

expedition	a trip that people take with a particular goal in mind
Gold Rush	the discovery of gold in California that brought 300,000 people to California in the mid-1800s
prairie schooners	wagons used on the plains that looked like ships in the grass
Homestead Act	a law that encouraged settlers to move to the western United States by giving a person free land in the west
homestead	the home and land a family owns
prairie	a grassy area with no trees
Transcontinental Railroad	a railroad built in the mid-1800s that connected the Atlantic and Pacific coasts of the United States for the first time
Oregon Trail	a wagon route used by pioneers moving to the West

Name _____

Westward Expansion Learning Contract

Directions: Choose at least two activities to complete from the list below. Fill in your project choices at the bottom of this sheet. Sign your contract and then ask your teacher to sign it, too. Use books or websites on westward expansion to help you complete the activities.

1. What is the Homestead Act? How did this act affect Americans? Why did the government create this act? After answering these questions, write a newspaper article from 1862 explaining the act to readers and predicting how this might affect the United States.

2. Pretend you are actually experiencing the Oregon Trail with your family. Your family is headed west in search of a better life. Create a diary and make six entries that will describe your adventure. Use historical facts in all of your entries. You may add drawings or sketches to your diary. You will need at least six entries that describe the beginning, middle, and end of your family's journey.

3. Find out how all of these words are related: *Gold Rush, bonanza, Forty-Niners, Comstock Lode, immigrants, boomtowns,* and *ghost town.* Pretend that you could interview someone from that time period. Write interview questions that show the significant history that surrounds these words.

4. Study the mining methods of the Gold Rush era and then study the environmental impact that mining had during the Gold Rush (panning, windlass and shaft, hydraulic mining, and cradle mining). Prepare a mini-booklet using index cards that shows what you have learned about mining gold back then.

5. Create a diagram, flow chart, or three-dimensional model to demonstrate some mechanical or engineering aspect of the Transcontinental Railroad that interests you.

I agree to complete the following two activities:

Activity 1: _____

Activity 2: _____

Due Date: _____

Student Signature: _____

Teacher Signature: _____

Name _____

Westward Expansion Learning Contract

Directions: Choose at least two activities to complete from the list below. Fill in your project choices at the bottom of this sheet. Sign your contract and then ask your teacher to sign it, too. Use books or websites on westward expansion to help you complete the activities.

1. Make a map that shows what the United States looked like at the time of westward expansion. Show where the following were located on the map: Oregon Trail, Mormon Trail, Transcontinental Railroad, Santa Fe Trail, Pony Express, and Lewis and Clark's expedition.

2. Make a mining town diorama. Construct a shoe box diorama of a gold town. Include miners' camps, staked-out claims, and various mining techniques.

3. The Homestead Act encouraged people to settle the land. Make a collage of at least eight pictures that shows exactly why the Homestead Act made people want to settle the land.

4. Find out what gold fever was. Write a commercial that informs others about gold fever. Either videotape the commercial or perform it live for your class.

5. How did the Transcontinental Railroad affect Americans? How did it affect wildlife like the bison? Show a conversation between bison and an American living at the time. This conversation should explain how the railroad affected both sides.

I agree to complete the following two activities:

Activity 1: _____

Activity 2: _____

Due Date: _____

Student Signature: _____

Teacher Signature: _____

Name _____

Westward Expansion Learning Contract

Directions: Choose at least two activities to complete from the list below. Fill in your project choices at the bottom of this sheet. Sign your contract and then ask your teacher to sign it, too. Use books or websites on westward expansion to help you complete the activities.

1. Make a map that shows what the United States looked like at the time of westward expansion. Show the Oregon Trail, the Santa Fe Trail, the Mormon Trail, and Lewis and Clark's expedition.

2. Covered wagons were the main way Americans were able to travel during the time of westward expansion. Find out what these wagons looked like, and how pioneers organized their belongings inside for the journey. Make a diagram of a covered wagon and label all the parts.

3. Make a mining town map. Show the many features of a gold town on this map. Include miners' camps, staked-out claims, and various mining techniques.

4. Today, it might be hard to understand why men left their homes and loved ones and traveled thousands of miles to look for gold. But in 1849, a prosperous farmer might make about two or three hundred dollars a year. A factory worker made about a dollar for working 12 hours a day. A skilled craftsman made a dollar and a half a day. How are things different today? Make a poster that compares these earnings with what people earn today.

5. Make a picture time line that identifies the important events in the making of the Transcontinental Railroad. Your time line should begin in 1865 and end in 1880.

I agree to complete the following two activities:

Activity 1: _____

Activity 2: _____

Due Date: _____

Student Signature: _____

Teacher Signature: _____

The Civil War

Differentiation Strategy

 Tiered Assignments

Standards

- Students will understand the technological, social, and strategic aspects of the Civil War.

- TESOL: Students will use appropriate learning strategies to construct and apply academic knowledge.

Materials

- lesson resources (pages 156–159)

- magnifying lenses

Procedures

Note: This lesson, which focuses on the first battle of the Civil War (Fort Sumter), works as an excellent introduction to a Civil War unit.

❶ Display the *Fort Sumter Map* activity sheet (page 156) and distribute copies to students. Allow students to use magnifying lenses so that they can read the fine print and see the small images on the map.

❷ Explain that this map shows the location of the first battle of the Civil War. Tell students to pretend that they are historians who discovered this map. What are some things that they notice about it? What seems important on this map? Have students think-pair-share about these two questions. Allow several students to share their thoughts with the class.

❸ Distribute copies of *The Beginning of the Civil War* activity sheets (pages 157–159) to students based on their readiness levels.

❹ Allow your above-grade-level students to work independently and your on-grade-level students to work with partners. Meet in a small group with your below-grade-level students.

★ **English Language Support**—These learners will be at all levels, and some need more challenging questions. However, the language will need to be adjusted. Choose the higher level questions from the square and triangle activity sheets, but simplify the language for these learners. If possible, have another adult or volunteer work with these students, reading the questions aloud to them.

❺ Provide students enough time to complete their questions. Then, tell the class that they will find partners with a different activity sheet. Students should sit facing their partner, and read the first question and answer from their activity sheet. Then, use a cue, such as flickering the lights or ringing a bell, to indicate that students should switch partners. With their second partners, students should each share their second question and answer. Repeat this four times so students can share all of their responses.

❻ Finally, provide students with the background on this famous battle.

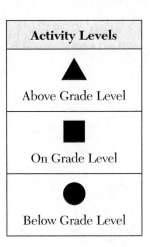

Activity Levels
▲ Above Grade Level
■ On Grade Level
● Below Grade Level

> South Carolina had just seceded from the Union. Union forces were stationed on Fort Sumter. Union General Anderson made the decision to move his troops there. Confederate General Beauregard was in Charlestown, South Carolina. He demanded that General Anderson surrender the fort to the Confederates. Anderson refused to surrender. The battle began at Fort Sumter on April 12, 1861. The Confederates bombarded the fort, and after just 34 hours, Anderson surrendered and the Confederates won. The Union Army left the fort. No one died in the battle.

❼ If students finish early, they may complete the Anchor Activity.

Assessment

Evaluate students' responses on their activity sheets to be sure you are assigning them the appropriate leveled work. Make notes on any necessary adjustments for future differentiated assignments.

Anchor Activity

Have students conduct additional research on Fort Sumter. They can create a filmstrip showing what took place there to accompany the map.

Name _____

Fort Sumter Map

Directions: Use the map below to answer the questions on your activity sheet.

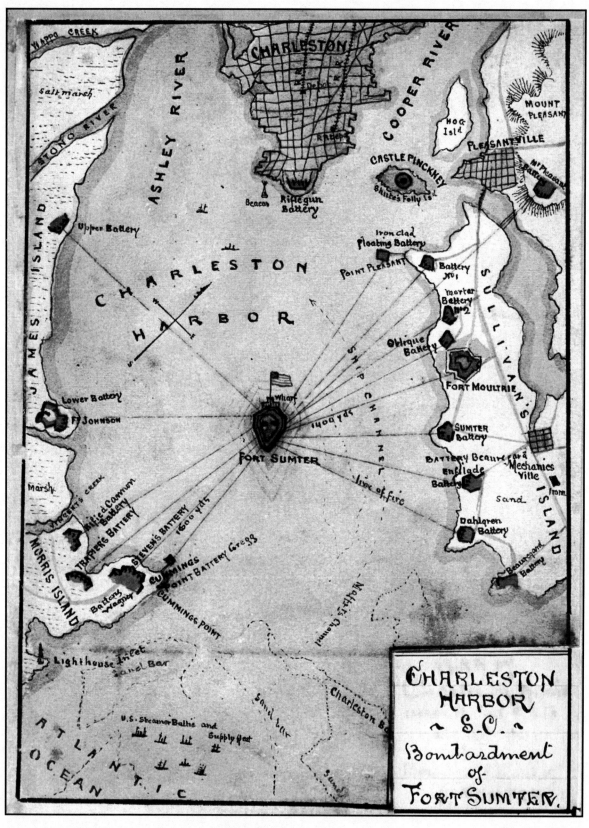

Name _____

The Beginning of the Civil War

Directions: Use the *Fort Sumter Map* to answer the questions below.

1. South Carolina had just seceded from the Union. Why do you think the Union general decided on his own to move his troops to Fort Sumter, right off the coast of South Carolina? What was his motive?

   _____

   _____

   _____

   _____

   _____

2. What evidence can you find on this map that tells who won this battle? Explain.

   _____

   _____

   _____

   _____

3. If you were President Lincoln, what orders would you give the general at Fort Sumter? Explain.

   _____

   _____

   _____

   _____

4. In what ways is this harbor a terrible location for a fort? One the other hand, why would it be ideal?

   _____

   _____

   _____

   _____

   _____

   _____

Name _____

The Beginning of the Civil War

Directions: Use the *Fort Sumter Map* to answer the questions below.

1. Explain what is happening on this map.

_____

_____

_____

_____

2. Look closely at the map. Who has a better chance of winning this battle? Explain.

_____

_____

_____

_____

_____

3. South Carolina had just seceded from the Union. Why do you think the Union general decided on his own to move his troops to Fort Sumter, right off the coast of South Carolina?

_____

_____

_____

_____

4. In what ways is this harbor a good location for a fort? In what ways is the harbor a bad location for this fort?

_____

_____

_____

_____

_____

Name _____

The Beginning of the Civil War

Directions: Use the *Fort Sumter Map* to answer the questions below.

1. Who is on the tiny island of Fort Sumter: the Union Army or the Confederate Army?

   _____

2. How do you know which army is on Fort Sumter?

   _____

   _____

3. Pretend you were on Fort Sumter. How does the map show that it would be hard to win the battle?

   _____

   _____

   _____

   _____

   _____

   _____

   _____

4. What would you recommend that the army on Fort Sumter do?

   _____

   _____

   _____

   _____

   _____

Reconstruction

Differentiation Strategy

Bloom's Taxonomy

Standards

- Students will understand military, political, and social factors affecting the post-Civil War period.

- TESOL: Students will use appropriate learning strategies to construct and apply academic knowledge.

Materials

- lesson resources (pages 162–165)

- chart paper and markers

Procedures

❶ Display *The Fifteenth Amendment* activity sheet (page 162) and distribute copies to students.

❷ Ask the following discussion questions about the image.

- Why do you think things like marriage, school, and church are included in a painting about the Fifteenth Amendment?

- Do you think the artist, Thomas Kelly, was Caucasian or an African American man? Why?

- What is the tone of this painting? What sets that tone?

❸ Distribute copies of *Reconstruction and the Fifteenth Amendment Background Information* activity sheet (page 163) to students. Read the information aloud to the class as they follow along.

★ **English Language Support**—Be sure to stop often while reading and summarize, clarify, and answer students' questions. Be sure that all students are grasping the background information. Answer any questions that students may have.

❹ Review the ideas and events of Congress's Reconstruction Plan. Allow students to come up and write these events on the board or chart paper.

Reconstruction

5 Tell students that they will be answering some questions based on the image that celebrates the Fifteenth Amendment. Distribute copies of the *Reconstruction Questions* activity sheet (page 164) to students.

6 Assign the questions to students based on their readiness levels.

△ **Evaluating and Creating**
above-grade-level students

□ **Applying and Analyzing**
on-grade-level students

◯ **Remembering and Understanding**
below-grade-level students

If students would like to try a different question, allow them to answer those other questions for extra credit.

7 Bring the class together to summarize their learning.

8 If students finish early, they may complete the Anchor Activity.

Assessment

Use the document-based assessment *The First Vote* (page 165) to evaluate what students have learned

Anchor Activity

Have students write a song that celebrates the many victories of Congressional Reconstruction, especially the Fifteenth Amendment.

The Fifteenth Amendment

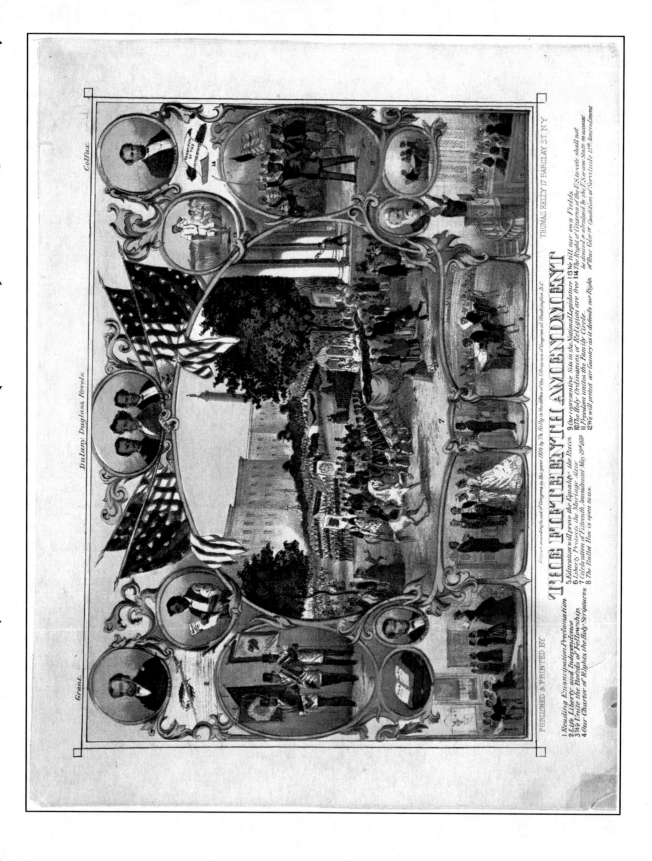

Name _____

Reconstruction and the Fifteenth Amendment Background Information

Directions: Read the background information below.

At the beginning of Reconstruction, the Republican Party controlled Congress. Republicans wanted to change Southern society completely. President Andrew Johnson fought these changes. Johnson was a Southerner, and he supported states' rights. He wanted each state to decide its own future. Congress was able to override, or overrule, the president. Congressional Reconstruction brought dramatic changes to the South. Sadly, those changes did not last.

In 1866, Republicans in Congress passed several bills to help freed slaves. Some of the bills helped the Freedmen's Bureau. Another bill was the first Civil Rights Act. This act made African Americans full citizens of the United States. The next success for Congress was the Fourteenth Amendment. This amendment said that laws had to protect African Americans the same way white people were protected. It banned racist laws like the Black Codes.

In 1867, Congress passed the Reconstruction Act. The act split the South into five military districts. Federal troops had to made sure that Southerners followed the new laws. The troops also made sure that elections were fair. For the first time in U.S. history, white men and African American men voted in the same elections. It was an exciting time for African Americans.

This was also a time of violence. In 1866, a mob attacked the Louisiana Constitutional Convention. Some people were angry that Republicans were changing Louisiana's laws. To Congress, riots like these proved that the South had a long way to go.

The main goal of Reconstruction was to bring the Southern states back into the Union. The South also wanted to have representatives in Congress. To do that, states had to ratify, or accept, new state constitutions. They also had to ratify the Thirteenth and Fourteenth Amendments. By June of 1868, most Southern states had rejoined the Union.

At this time, African Americans still could not vote in the North. It was also hard for African Americans to cast ballots in the South. In 1869, Congress passed the Fifteenth Amendment. This gave all men the right to vote, regardless of color or race. By 1870, all Southern states had agreed to support the Fifteenth Amendment. The United States was finally made whole again.

The success of Congressional Reconstruction was short-lived. By the early 1900s, Southern states found new ways to rob African Americans of basic rights. Another Civil Rights Act was passed in the 1960s. It protected the rights of African Americans and women.

Name _____

Reconstruction Questions

Directions: Use a separate sheet of paper to answer the questions below. Answer the questions assigned by your teacher.

Remembering

The Thirteenth, Fourteenth, and Fifteenth amendments gave African Americans rights which they never had before in the United States. Design a simple symbol, or logo, to represent each amendment. People should be able to understand the main idea of each amendment from your drawings.

Understanding

The image on *The Fifteenth Amendment* activity sheet (page 162) depicts all of the areas of African American life affected by the Fifteenth Amendment. How did having the right to vote impact marriage, work, church life, schooling, and other aspects of daily life? Choose three areas and explain how voting rights made an impact.

Applying

Imagine that you are in the audience pictured at the center of the image on *The Fifteenth Amendment* activity sheet (page 162). You are an African American celebrating the passage of the Fifteenth Amendment. Write a diary entry describing what you saw and how you felt about the day's events.

Analyzing

Why do you think African Americans got the right to vote in Southern states before they got the same right in many Northern states? Explain your answer.

Evaluating

There were many different ideas about how to rebuild the nation after the war. Imagine that you were a Northern senator during Reconstruction. Which plan would you have supported? Explain your choice.

Creating

Congressional Reconstruction was a plan with lofty goals. The process of making it happen was painful, deadly, and unsuccessful. Would the use of modern technology have changed Congressional Reconstruction? Would technology have made it more successful in the end? Choose three modern technologies and describe how they could have been used during Reconstruction. Then, explain how they might have changed the process of rebuilding the nation.

The First Vote

Directions: Answer the following questions about this illustration.

1. What do you think the man is putting in the jar?

   _____

2. How do you think the men in the photo felt about what they were doing?

   _____

   _____

3. The Fifteenth Amendment gave African American men the right to vote. Why do you think that is considered one of only a few successes of Reconstruction?

   _____

   _____

   _____

Anderson, L. W., and D. R. Krathwohl, eds. 2001. *A taxonomy for learning, teaching, and assessing: A revision of Bloom's taxonomy of educational objectives.* Boston: Allyn and Bacon.

Bess, J. 1997. *Teaching well and liking it: Motivating faculty to teach effectively.* Baltimore, MD: Johns Hopkins University Press.

Bloom, B. S. and D. R. Krathwohl. 1984. *Taxonomy of educational objectives: Handbook I; Cognitive Domain.* White Plains, NY: Longman.

Brandt, R. 1998. *Powerful learning.* Alexandria, VA: Association for Supervision and Curriculum Development.

Bruner, J. 2004. *Toward a theory of instruction.* Cambridge, MA: Belnap Press of Harvard University Press.

Costa, A. L., and R. Marzano. 1987. Teaching the language of thinking. *Educational Leadership* 45: 29–33.

Gardner, H. 1983. *Frames of mind: The theory of multiple intelligences.* New York: Basic Books.

———. 1999. *Intelligence reframed: Multiple intelligences for the 21st Century.* New York: Basic Books.

Jensen, E. 1998. *Teaching with the brain in mind.* Alexandria, VA: Association for Supervision and Curriculum Development.

Kaplan, S. N. 2001. Layering differentiated curriculum for the gifted and talented. In *Methods and materials for teaching the gifted*, ed. F. Karnes and S. Bean, 133–158. Waco, TX: Prufrock Press.

Olsen, K. D. 1995. *Science continuum of concepts: For grades K–6.* Black Diamond, WA: Books for Educators.

Sprenger, M. 1999. *Learning and memory: The brain in action.* Alexandria, VA: Association for Supervision and Curriculum Development.

Teele, S. 1994. Redesigning the educational system to enable all students to succeed. PhD Diss., University of California, Riverside.

Winebrenner, S. 1992. *Teaching gifted kids in the regular classroom.* Minneapolis, MN: Free Spirit Publishing.

Additional Resources

Where books and websites are referenced in lesson materials lists, some suggestions for these resources are provided below. Shell Education does not control the content of these websites, or guarantee their ongoing availability, or links contained therein. We encourage teachers to preview these websites before directing students to use them.

Page 22—Identifying Genres

www.bpl.org/kids.booksmags.htm

www.mainlesson.com/displaybooksbygenre.php

www.plcmc.org/bookhive/books/

Page 52—Making Inferences

www.imdb.com

www.movieclips.com

Page 70—Equivalent Fractions

McMillan, Bruce. *Eating Fractions.* New York: Scholastic, 1991.

Murphy, Stewart J. *Give Me Half!* New York: HarperCollins, 1996.

Page 82—Geometry Wrap-Up

Escher, M. C. *M. C. Escher: The Graphic Work* (Special Edition) Köln, Germany: Taschen, 2008.

Biddle, Steve and Megumi Biddle. *Origami: Inspired by Japanese Prints from the Metropolitan Museum of Art.* New York: Viking, 1998.

www.mcescher.com

www.origami-instructions.com

Page 106—Food Chains

Davis, Barbara J. *Biomes and Ecosystems.* New York: Gareth Stevens Publishing, 2007.

Pipe, Jim. *Earth's Ecosystems.* New York: Gareth Stevens Publishing, 2008.

Wallace, Marianne D. *America's Wetlands: Guide to Plants and Animals.* Golden, CO: Fulcrum Publishing, 2004.

www.nationalgeographic.com

www.nwf.org/kids

Page 118—Animal Adaptations

Crossingham, John and Bobbie Kalman. *What Are Camouflage and Mimicry?* New York: Crabtree Publishing Company, 2001.

Kalman, Bobbie and Niki Walker. *How Do Animals Adapt?* New York: Crabtree Publishing Company, 2000.

Slade, Suzanne. *What Do You Know About Animal Adaptations?* New York: PowerKids Press, 2008.

www.animal.discovery.com

Page 124—Forces and Motion

www.nasa.gov

www.neok12.com/Laws-of-Motion.htm

www.pbskids.org/dragonflytv/show/mattermotion.html

Page 130—Colonial America

Englar, Mary. *Dutch Colonies in America.* Mankato, MN: Compass Point Books, 2008.

Lilly, Alexandra. *Spanish Colonies in America.* Mankato, MN: Compass Point Books, 2008.

Maestro, Betsy. *The New Americans: Colonial Times; 1620–1689.* New York: HarperColllins, 2004.

www.history.com

www.history.org/kids

Page 136—Revolutionary Social Networking

Moore, Kay. *If You Lived at the Time of the American Revolution.* New York: Scholastic, 1997.

Murray, Stuart. *American Revolution.* New York: DK Publishing, 2005.

www.history.com

Page 148—Westward Expansion

Erickson, Paul. *Daily Life in a Covered Wagon.* New York: Puffin Books, 1994.

George, Lynn. *What Do You Know About Westward Expansion?* New York: PowerKids Press, 2008.

www.pbs.org/weta/thewest/resources/archives

Contents of the Teacher Resource CD

Lesson Resource Pages

Page	Lesson	Filename
24–27	Identifying Genres	pg024.pdf
30–33	Writing with Details	pg030.pdf
36–39	Persuasive Practice	pg036.pdf
42–45	Literature Response	pg042.pdf
48–51	Book in a Day	pg048.pdf
54–57	Making Inferences	pg054.pdf
60–63	Number Sense	pg060.pdf
66–69	Long Division Algorithm	pg066.pdf
72–75	Equivalent Fractions	pg072.pdf
78–81	Exploring Volume	pg078.pdf
84–87	Geometry Wrap-Up	pg084.pdf
90–93	Introducing Algebra	pg090.pdf
96–99	The Scientific Method	pg096.pdf
102–105	Rock Investigation	pg102.pdf
108–111	Food Chains	pg108.pdf
114–117	Inherited Traits	pg114.pdf
120–123	Animal Adaptations	pg120.pdf
126–129	Forces and Motion	pg126.pdf
132–135	Colonial America	pg132.pdf
138–141	Revolutionary Social Networking	pg138.pdf
144–147	Declaration of Independence	pg144.pdf
150–153	Westward Expansion	pg150.pdf
156–159	The Civil War	pg156.pdf
162–165	Reconstruction	pg162.pdf

Image Resources

Page	Image	Filename
54	Virginia Quarter	quarter.jpg
55	Valley Forge	valleyforge.jpg
56	Beach	beach.jpg
106	Fox	fox.pdf
106	Grass	grass.pdf
106	Hawk	hawk.pdf
106	Rabbit	rabbit.pdf
106	Snake	snake.pdf
106	Sun	sun.pdf
138	Benjamin Franklin	franklin.jpg
138	George Washington	gwashington.jpg
138	John Hancock	hancock.jpg
138	Martha Washington	mwashington.jpg
138	Paul Revere	revere.jpg

Teacher Resources

Title	Filename
Answer Key	answers.pdf
Bingo Board	bingo.pdf
Comic Strip	comic.pdf
Flow Chart	flow.pdf
T-Chart	tchart.pdf
Three Column Chart	threecolumn.pdf
Time Line	timeline.pdf
Triple Venn Diagram	triplevenn.pdf
Venn Diagram	venn.pdf